Reading Mastery II   Fast Cycle

Storybook 2

Siegfried Engelmann
Elaine C. Bruner

Macmillan/McGraw-Hill

ISBN: 0-574-10153-5

6 7 8 9 10 RRC 99 98 97 96 95 94 93 92

Contents

arf the shark

arf was a barkiñg shark. arf was a littlₑ shark, but shē had a big bark that mādₑ the other fish swim awāy.

a shark swam up to arf and said, "you arₑ a shark. let's plāy."

arf was happy. "arf, arf," shē said. and the other shark swam far, far awāy. arf was not happy now.

another shark swam up to arf. "you arₑ a shark," hē said. "let's plāy."

arf was happy. "arf, arf," shē said. and the other shark

swam far, far awāy. arf was
not happy now.

then a big, big fish that līked
to ēat sharks swam up to the
other sharks.

"help, help," they yelled.

but the big fish was
swimmiñg after them very fast.

stop

arf can help

arf was a barking shark. the other sharks did not līke her big bark. when arf went "arf, arf," the other sharks swam awāy.

but now arf had to help the other sharks. a big fish that līked to ēat sharks was gōing after the other sharks. arf swam up to the big fish and said, "arf, arf." the big fish swam far, far awāy.

the other sharks līked arf now.

"wē līke arf now," they said.

and now arf plāys with the other sharks. and if a big fish

that līkes to ēat sharks swims
up to them, arf says "arf, arf."
and the big fish swims far, far
awāy.

the end

rēad the Ītems

1. when the tēacher stands up,
   sāy "you arₑ standiñg up."
2. when the tēacher claps, pick
   up your book.

spot

this is a stōry of a dog
nāmₑd spot. spot did not hēar
well. the other dāy shē went to
a stōrₑ to get some bōnₑs. the
man in the stōrₑ said, "it is a
fīnₑ dāy."

"what did you sāy?" spot
askₑd.

tell spot what the man said.

the man got some bōnes fōr
spot. hē said, "pāy mē a dīme
fōr thēse bōnes."

spot askeḏ, "what did you
sāy?"

tell spot what the man said.

spot did not hēar the man
and the man was gettiñg mad at
spot. the man said, "give mē a
dīme fōr thēse bōnes."

spot askeḏ, "what did you
sāy?"

tell spot what the man said.

spot said, "it is tīme fōr mē
to lēave. sō I will pāy you a
dīme fōr the bōnes and I will
gō hōme."

sō spot gāve the man a dīme.

then shē took the bōnes hōme

and had a fīne mēal of bōnes.

the end

rēad the Ītem

when the tēacher says "now,"
clap.

the dog līkes to talk, talk, talk

a tall man had a dog that
līked to talk and līked to rēad.

one dāy the dog was rēading
a book. the tall man was in the
hall. he called the dog. he yelled,
"dog, come hēre and plāy ball
with me."

the dog yelled back at the
man, "I hēar you call, call, call,
but I dōn't līke to plāy ball,
ball, ball."

the man was getting mad. he
yelled, "dog, stop rēading that
book and start plāying ball."

she yelled, "I will not go
into the hall, hall, hall, and I will
not plāy ball, ball, ball."

the man was very mad now.
he cāme into the room and got
his cōat. he said, "well, I am
gōing for a walk. do you want to
come with me?"

the dog said, "I will not do
that, that, that, when I can sit
hēre and get fat, fat, fat."

so the tall man left and the
dog went back to her book.
she said, "I hāte to walk, walk,

9

walk, but I līk_e to talk, talk, talk."

the end

rēₐd the Ītem

when the tēₐcher says "do it,"
hōld up your hand.

the small bug went to
livₑ in a ball

therₑ was a small bug that
did not havₑ a hōmₑ. he went to
livₑ in a tall trēē. but a big
ēₐglₑ said, "this is mȳ tall trēē.
go look for another hōmₑ."

then the bug livₑd in a hōlₑ.
but a mōlₑ said, "that's mȳ
hōlₑ. go look for another hōmₑ."

then the small bug livₑd on a
farm in a box of salt. but a cow

said, "that's mȳ salt. go awāy or I'll ēat you up when I lick mȳ salt."

then the small bug livₑd in a stall on the farm. but a hōrsₑ said, "what arₑ you doiñg in mȳ stall? go fīnd another hōmₑ."

at last the bug went to a hōmₑ nēar the farm. he spotted a ball on the flōōr. the ball had a small hōlₑ in it. the bug said, "at last I sēē a hōmₑ for me." he went into the ball and sat down. he said, "I hōpₑ that I can stāy in this ball. I līkₑ it hērₑ."

mōrₑ to come

rēad the Ītem

when the tēₐcher says "go," sāy "stand up."

the bug in the ball mēēts a girl

a small bug had a hōmₑ in a ball. he said, "I hōpₑ I can stāy in this ball. I lĪkₑ it hērₑ."

he went to slēēp in the ball. he was havin͡g a good drēₐm. he was drēₐmin͡g of a fĪnₑ party. then he sat up. the ball was rōllin͡g. "what is gōin͡g on?" he callₑd.

he lookₑd from the littlₑ hōlₑ in the ball and saw a tall

girl. she was rōlling the ball on the flōōr.

"what are you doing?" he asked. "this is mȳ hōme. stop rōlling it on the flōōr."

the girl picked up the ball and looked at the small bug. then she dropped the ball. "ōh," she crĪed, "there is a bug in mȳ ball. I hāte bugs."

the ball hit the flōōr. it went up. then it went down. then it went up. the bug was getting sick.

"stop that," he called. "I dōn't lĪke a hōme that gōes up and down."

the tall girl bent down and
looked at the bug. she said,
"this is mȳ ball. so go awāy."
 the small bug looked up at
the girl and started to crȳ.
mōre to come

rēₐd the Ītem

when the tēₐcher stands up, sāy "you arₑ standiñg up."

the buǥ wants to stāy
in the ball

a small buǥ wanted to livₑ insĪdₑ a ball. but a tall girl tōld him that he must lēₐvₑ the ball and fĪnd another hōmₑ. the small buǥ started to crȳ. he said, "wherₑ will I go? I cannot livₑ in a tall trēē. I cannot livₑ in a box of salt. I cannot livₑ in a hōrsₑ stall. and now I cannot stāy in this ball."

"stop cr͞yin͡g," the girl said.
"I can't stand to se͞e small bugs
cr͞y."

the bug said, "if you let me
st͞ay in this ball, I will pl͞ay with
you."

"no," the girl said. "I d͞on't
pl͞ay with bugs. I h͞ate bugs."

the bug said, "I can sin͡g for
you. I will ͞even let you come to
the party that I am g͞oin͡g to
hav_e in m͞y ball."

she said, "d͞on't be silly. I
can't fit in that ball. look at
how tall I am."

the bug call_ed, "let me st͞ay."
the girl sat down on the

flōor and lookₑd at the small
bug. "I must think," she said.
what was she gōing to think
ōver?

more to come

rēₐd the Ītem

when the tēₐcher says "go,"
touch your arm.

the tall girl bets her
brother

a tall girl wanted the bug to
lēₐve the ball and fĪnd another
hōme. the bug crĪₑd and tōld
her all the thiñgs he would do if
she let him stāy in the ball. he
said that he would siñg for her.
he said that he would let her
come to his party in the ball.

the girl was sittiñg on the
flōōr thinkiñg of the bug.

then her brother cāme into
the room. he said, "what arₑ you
doin͡g?"

she said, "go awāy. I am
thinkin͡g."

he said, "do you think that
the ball will start rōllin͡g if you
look at it very hard?" her
brother did not sēē the bug
insῙdₑ the ball.

the girl said, "if I want this
ball to start rōllin͡g, it will
start rōllin͡g. and I dōn't ēven
havₑ to touch it."

her brother said, "I'll bet
you can't mākₑ that ball rōll
if you dōn't touch it."

"how much will you bet?" the
girl asked. she looked at the
bug and smīled.

her brother said, "I will bet
you one football and ten toy
cars."

the girl said, "I will tāke
that bet."

mōre to come

rēₐd the Ītem

when the tēₐcher says "stop,"
touch the flōōr.

the tall girl wins the bet

the tall girl mādₑ a bet with
her brother. she bet him that she
could mākₑ the ball start rōlliñg.
she said, "I dōn't ēven havₑ to
touch it."

her brother did not sēē the
bug in the ball. so he bet one
football and ten toy cars.

the girl lookₑd at the ball and
said, "start rōlliñg, ball." the

bug started runnin͡g insIde the ball. he ran and ran. he ran so fast that the ball started to rōll.

the girl's brother lookeᴅ at the ball. he said, "wow. that ball is rōllin͡g and you areꜱ not ēven touchin͡g it."

the girl said, "I tōld you I could māke the ball rōll."

so the girl got one football and ten toy cars.

then she said to the small bug, "you helpeᴅ me win the bet, so I will let you stāy in mȳ ball. this ball is your hōme now."

the bug was so happy that he ran from the ball and kisseᴅ

the girl on her hand. "thank you, thank you," he said.

and nēar the end of the wēēk, he had a fīne party insīde his ball. every bug on the strēēt cāme to the party, and they all said that it was the very best party they ever had.

the end

the dog loves to rēad, rēad, rēad

a dog that could talk livₑd with a tall man. the dog took a book from the tābl. the dog said, "this book is whₐt I nēēd, nēēd, nēēd. I love to rēad, rēad, rēad."

the tall man cāmₑ in and said, "I look, look, look, but I cannot sēē mȳ book, book, book."

then the man said, "mȳ book was on the tābl."

the dog said, "the book was on the tābl, but I took it from the tābl."

the tall man yellₑd at the dog.

he said, "you must not tāke mȳ book from the tābl₆."

she said, "do you want to plāy ball, ball, ball in the hall, hall, hall?"

"yes, yes," the man said.

the dog kick₆d the ball far, far, far down the hall. when the man ran after the ball, the dog took the book and hid it.

then she said, "let the man look, look, look. he will never fīnd his book, book, book."

the end

30

walter wanted to plāy football

walter loved to plāy football. but walter could not plāy well. he was small. and he did not run well. when he trīed to run with the ball, he fell down. "dōn't fall down," the other boys yelled. but walter kept fallíng and fallíng.

when walter ran to get a pass, he dropped the football. "dōn't drop the ball," the other boys yelled. but walter kept droppíng balls.

dāy after dāy walter trīed to plāy football, but dāy after dāy he fell down and dropped the ball.

then one dāy, the other boys said, "walter, you can't plāy ball with us any mōre. you are too small.

you alwāys fall. and you alwāys
drop the football."

walter went hōme and sat in his
yard. he was mad. he said to himself,
"I am small and I cannot run well."
walter wanted to crȳ, but he
didn't crȳ. he sat in his yard
and felt very sad. when his mom
called him for dinner, he said, "I
dōn't want to ēat. I must sit hēre
and think."

more to come

walter gōes to the big gāme

walter was sad bēcause the other boys would not let him plāy football with them. walter was still sad on the dāy of the big football gāme. the boys that lived nēar walter wer‌e plāyinģ boys from the other sīde of town.

walter went down to the lot wher‌e the boys plāy football. he said, "I can't plāy in the gāme bēcause I alwāys fall. but I will look at the big gāme."

ther‌e wer‌e lots of boys and girls at the football lot. some of them wer‌e chēērinģ for the boys that lived nēar walter. other boys and girls wer‌e chēērinģ for the tēam that cāme from the other sīde of town.

34

the gāme started. there was a tall
boy on the other tēam. that tall boy
got the football and ran all the wāy
down the lot. he scōred. the boys
and girls from the other sīde of
town chēēred.

walter's tēam got the ball. but
they could not go far. they went
fīve yards.

when the other tēam got the ball,
the tall boy kicked the ball. it went
to the end of the lot for another
scōre. walter said to himself, "that
other tēam is gōiñg to win. I wish
I could help mȳ tēam."

mōre to come

walter gōes in the gāme

walter was looking at the big football gāme. walter's tēam was not doing well. the other tēam had 2 scōres. but walter's tēam did not have any scōres. as the gāme went on, walter's tēam started to plāy well. walter's tēam stopped the tall boy when he got the ball. then walter's tēam scōred. walter chēēred. he yelled, "get that ball and scōre some mōre."

but then the best plāyer on walter's tēam cut his arm. he left the gāme. walter said to himself, "now we cannot win the gāme. the best plāyer is not plāying."

how could walter's tēam win if the best plāyer was not plāying?

then all the boys on walter's tēam started to call. "walter, walter," they called. "come hēre."

walter ran to his tēam. one of the boys said, "walter, we nēēd one mōre plāyer. so we called you. trȳ to plāy well. we nēēd 2 scōres to win this gāme."

more to come

walter's tēam must kick

walter's tēam called him to plāy in the big gāme.

one of the boys on walter's tēam said, "we cannot run with the ball, bēcause the best runner is not in the gāme. so let's trȳ to scōre bȳ kickiñg the ball."

"yes, yes," the other boys said.

then the boys looked at ēach other. "one of us must kick the ball."

all the other boys said, "not me. I can't kick the ball that far."

but walter didn't sāy "no." he said, "I will trȳ. I think I could kick the ball that far."

one of the boys said, "I will hōld the ball for him."

so walter got re_a_dy to kick the
ball. some boys and girls call_e_d
from the sᾱde of the lot, "dōn't let
walter do that. he can't plāy football.
he will fall down."

but walter said to himself, "I will
not fall. I will kick that ball." and
walter felt that he would kick the
ball.

mōr_e_ to come

walter kicks the ball

walter was ready to kick the ball. the boys and girls on the sīde of the lot werе sāyiñg, "dōn't let walter kick."

but walter did kick. another boy held the ball. a tall boy from the other tēam almōst got to the ball, but walter kicked the ball just in tīme. the ball went līke a shot. it went past the end of the lot. it went ōver a tall wall that was next to the lot. it almōst hit a car that was on the strēēt.

the boys on walter's tēam looked at walter. the boys on the other tēam looked at walter. one boy from the other tēam said, "that ball went all the wāy ōver the wall. I did not think

that a small boy could kick a ball
so far."

the boys and girls on the sīde
of the lot chēēred. "that's the wāy
to kick, walter," they called.

now walter's tēam nēēded one
mōre scōre to win the gāme.

mōre to come

walter's tēam wins

the other tēam did not scōre. so walter's tēam got the ball.

one boy on walter's tēam said, "we must go all the wāy down the lot to scōre. but we dōn't have tīme and we can't kick the ball that far."

walter said, "I think I can kick the ball all the wāy." so the boys on walter's tēam got ready.

the ball went into plāy. a boy from walter's tēam held the ball, and walter kicked it. it went all the wāy to the end of the lot. it almōst hit the wall that was next to the lot.

the boys on walter's tēam picked him up and yelled, "walter kicked for a scōre." the boys from the other tēam said, "you are some football plāyer."

and the boys and girls on the sĪde of the lot called, "walter is the star of the gāme." walter was very happy.

and now walter can plāy football with the other boys any tĪme he wants.

the end

45

carmen the cow

this is a stōry about a cow
nāmed carmen.

when the other cows said "moo,"
the children alwāys cāme to pet
them. but when carmen said "moo,"
all the children alwāys ran awāy.
the children ran awāy bēcause
carmen had a loud moo. she trīed to
sāy a little moo, but her moo was
alwāys a big, loud moo.

the other cows made fun of her.
they said, "we do not līke you
bēcause your moo is so loud."

carmen trīed and trīed, but her
moo was too loud.

one dāy some children cāme to
the farm with a tēacher. they cāme
to pet the cows. they petted all the

other cows, but they did not pet
carmen bēcause they did not līke
her loud moo.

one of the children started to
run up a hill, but she fell in a
dēēp, dēēp hōle. she shouted for
help. but the tēacher did not hēar
her calls. the other cows trīed to
help her. they called "moo, moo,"
but the moos were not very loud, and
the tēacher did not hēar them.

mōre to come

carmen calls for help

who cāme to the farm to pet
cows?

whȳ didn't the children pet
carmen?

who fell into a dēēp, dēēp hōle?

how did the other cows trȳ to
help the girl?

whȳ didn't the tēacher hēar the
cows mooiñg?

then carmen saw the girl. carmen
called "moo" very loud. she called
"moo" so loud that the tēacher could
hēar her. the tēacher said, "that
sounds līke a call for help." the
tēacher ran to the little girl.

the tēacher helped the little girl
get out of the hōle. the tēacher went
ōver to carmen and said, "we are so

glad that you have a loud moo. you said 'moo' so loud that you sāved the little girl."

and what do you think the little girl did? the little girl kissed carmen and said, "thank you for mooing so loud."

now carmen has lots of children pet her. carmen is happy that she has a big, loud moo.

this is the end.

1

the magic pouch

ther_e was a little girl who lived
nēar a tall mountain. the mountain
was so tall that the top was alwāys
in the clouds. the girl wanted to
go to the top of the mountain, but
her mother tōld her, "no." she said,
"that mountain is stēēp. you would
fīnd it very hard to get to the top."

but one dāy the little girl was
sitting and looking at the mountain.
she said to herself, "I would līke to
see what is in thōse clouds at the
top of the mountain. I think I
will go up and see."

so the girl took her pet hound
and started up the tall mountain.
they went up and up. the sīde of

the mountain was very stēēp. up
they went. the girl said to her
hound, "do not fall. it is very far
down to the ground."

soon the little girl and her
hound cāme to the clouds nēar the
top of the mountain. she said to her
hound, "now we will see what is on
the other sīde of thōse clouds."

what do you think they will see
on the other sīde of the clouds?

mōre to come

2

the magic pouch

where did the little girl live?

what did the girl want to do?

who tōld her not to go up the mountain?

who did she tāke with her?

where did the girl go with her hound?

the little girl and her hound went into the clouds. she said, "I cannot see too well. thēse clouds māke a fog." but the girl and her hound kept gōing up and up.

all at once they cāme out of the clouds. they could not see the ground any mōre. they could ōnly see clouds under them. they were in the sun. the sun was in the girl's eyes, so she could not see well. she sat down and said to her hound, "we must sit and rest."

all at once the little girl looked up and saw a funny little house. she said, "I didn't see that house before. let's go see who lives there."

so the girl and her hound walked over to the funny little house.

all at once a loud sound came from the house.

more to come

3

the magic pouch

where did the little girl and her hound go?

what did they see when they cāme out of the clouds?

what did they hēar comiñg from the house?

when the loud sound cāme from the house, the little girl stopped. she looked all around, but she did not see anyone. the sound cāme from the house once mōre. the girl and her hound walked up to the house. she called, "is anyone insīde that house?"

all at once the dōōr of the house ōpened. the girl looked insīde the house, but she did not see anyone. slōwly she walked insīde. slōwly her hound walked insīde. then the dōōr slammed bēhīnd them. the hound jumped. the girl jumped. she said, "let's get out of hēre." she grabbed the dōōr, but it would not ōpen. the girl said, "I dōn't līke this."

all at once the girl looked at a funny pouch hanging on the wall. and a loud sound cāme out of the pouch. it said, "ōpen this pouch and let me out."

mōre to come

4

the magic pouch

what did the little girl and her hound see on top of the mountain?

whȳ didn't they lēave the funny house?

what was hangin͞g on the wall?

the girl walked ōver to the pouch. she said, "is there some thin͞g in that pouch?"

"yes. I am a magic elf. I have lived in this pouch for a thousand yēars. plēase, would you ōpen the pouch and let me out?"

the little girl asked, "how many yēars have you lived in that pouch?"

the elf said, "a thousand yēars."

the girl started to ōpen the pouch. then she stopped. she said, "elf, I dōn't think I should let you out. this is not mȳ house. I should not be hēre."

the elf said, "this is mȳ house. so plēase ōpen the pouch and let me out. if you let me out, I will give you the pouch. it is magic."

the girl touched the pouch. she asked herself, "should I ōpen this pouch and let him out?"

more to come

5

the magic pouch

what was insIde the pouch?

how many yēars had the elf lived
in the pouch?

the little girl said to herself,
"should I ōpen this pouch?" she
looked at the pouch. then slōwly she
ōpened it. out jumped a little elf,
no bigger than your foot. the girl's
hound went, "owwwww." then the elf
jumped all around the room. he
jumped on the tāble and on the
flōōr. then he ran up one wall and
down the other wall. he ēven ran
around the hound. "owwwww," the
hound yelled.

"I'm out. I'm out," the elf
shouted. "I lived in that pouch a

thousand yēars and now I'm out."

at last the girl's hound stoppₑd gōīng "owwwww." the elf sat on the tāble and said, "I thank you very much. plēaₛe tāke the magic pouch. but be cāreful. when you arₑ good, the pouch will be good to you. but when you arₑ bad, the pouch will be bad to you.

mōrₑ to come

63

6

the magic pouch

the elf tōld the little girl, "when you are bad, the pouch will be bad to you."

the girl picked up the pouch. she said to the elf, "I have been good to you. let's see if this magic pouch will be good to me."

she rēached insIde the pouch and found ten round rocks that shIne. "thēse round rocks are gōld," she shouted. "I'm rich."

so the girl thanked the elf for the pouch.

then the girl and her hound started down the tall mountain. they went down and down. they went into the clouds. when they left the clouds, the girl could see the ground. down and down they went.

when they rēached the bottom of the mountain, the sun was setting. it was getting lāte. the girl was tīred. but she ran to her house.

her mother met her at the dōōr. she said, "where were you? your father and I have looked all around for you."

the little girl did not tell her mother where she went. she said, "I went to slēēp in the grass. I just wōke up." she tōld a līe, and that was bad.

mōre to come

7

the magic pouch

did the little girl tell her mother wher_e she was?

what did she tell her mother?

what does the pouch do when you ar_e bad?

the girl's mother look_ed at the pouch. she said, "wher_e did you get that pouch?"

"I found it on the ground," the little girl said. she tōld another lī_e. "but mother, ther_e ar_e ten rocks of gōld in this pouch. we ar_e rich."

she rē_ach_ed in the pouch and took somethin͞g out. but when she look_ed, she saw that she was not hōldin͞g gōld rocks. she was hōldin͞g yellōw mud. her mother said, "you ar_e not funny. we are not rich. but you are dirty. go clean your hands."

the little girl got a rag and trīed to rub the yellōw mud from her hands. but it would not come from her hands. she rubbed and rubbed, but the yellōw mud stāyed on her hands. her mother trīed to get the mud from her hands, but she could not do it.

then the girl started to crȳ.

mōre to come

8

the magic pouch

what did the little girl take from the pouch?

could she get the yellow mud from her hands?

could her mother get the yellow mud from her hands?

the girl cried and cried. then she said, "mother, I told you some lies. I did not sleep in the grass. I went to the top of the tall mountain. and I did not find the pouch on the ground. a funny elf gave it to me." the girl told her mother all about the funny house and the elf.

and when she looked at her hands, she saw that they were clean.

her mother said, "where did the mud go?"

"I dōn't see it any where," the girl said. she looked to see if there was more mud inside the pouch. and what do you think was inside the pouch? there were a thousand rocks of gōld. her mother said, "we are rich. we are very rich."

and the little girl said to herself, "that pouch is good to me because I was good. I will kēep on doing good things." and she did. and every time she was good, she rēached in the pouch and found something good.

no more to come

sam gets a kite kit

sam liked to make things. he liked to make toy cars. so he went to the store and got a toy car kit. his mom said, "that kit has the parts of a car. you have to rēad and fīnd out how to fit the parts so that they make a car."

sam said, "I will do that."

so sam began to rēad the pāper that came with the car kit. then he began to fit the parts to make a car. soon he had a toy car.

his mom said, "that is a fine car. you are good at rēading and at making things."

sam did not like to make the same thing again. he said, "I will not make other cars. I will make something else."

so he went to the store and got a kite kit. when he got home, he shōwed his mom the kite kit. his mom said, "that kit has a lot of parts in it. you will have to rēad the pāper that comes with the kit to fīnd out how to make the kite."

sam looked inside the kit. then he said, "what pāper? there is no pāper in this kit."

sam's mom said, "that is too bad. how will you make the kite if there is no pāper in the kit?"

sam said, "I will go back to the store and get a pāper that tells how to make a kite from these parts."

when sam got to the store, the man in the store said, "I dōn't have other pāpers that tell how to make kites."

sam asked, "how can I make a kite if I dōn't have the pāper?"

the man said, "you will have to do the best you can."

sam was not happy. he went home and looked at all the parts in the kite kit.

more to come

sam makes a funny kite

sam liked to make things. he had made a toy car from a kit. he did a good job. now sam had a kite kit. but there was no pāper in the kit to tell how to make a kite from the parts.

sam was not very happy. he looked at ēach of the parts. then he began to trȳ to make a kite from the parts in the kit. he worked and worked.

when his mom saw the kite, she said, "hō, hō. that is a funny-looking kite."

it was funny-looking. it looked like a small tent made out of pāper and wood. the top of the kite was very sharp.

77

sam's mom said, "I'm sorry for making fun of your kite, but it looks very funny."

sam said, "I dōn't care how funny it looks. I think it will flȳ."

his mom said, "no, I dōn't think it will. it does not look like a kite that will flȳ."

"we will see," sam said.

so sam and his mom went to the park. therₑ werₑ lots of boys and girls in the park. some of them werₑ flȳing kites. and some of the kites werₑ wāy up in the skȳ.

sam said, "I think mȳ kite will pass up all those kites."

sam's mom said, "I dōn't think your kite will go thrēē fēēt from the ground."

do you think sam's kite will flȳ?
more next time

can sam's kite rēally flȳ?

when sam made his kite, his mom said that it looked funny. so did the boys and girls in the park. they looked at the kite and said, "hō, hō, that thing looks like a tent. it wōn't flȳ."

sam said, "we will see."

sam's kite began to go up. up, up it went. it was going up very fast. sam's mom said, "well, would you look at that kite go up."

the boys and girls said, "wow, that kite can rēally flȳ."

soon sam's kite passed up all the other kites. it went up so far it looked like a little spot.

some of the boys and girls asked sam, "where did you get that kite?"

sam said, "you can get a kit for

this kite at the toy store. but I will have to tell you how to fit the parts so that they make a tent kite."

more and more boys and girls asked sam about his kite. at last sam said, "I will make a pāper that tells how to make a tent kite from the kit."

and he did. when he got home, he sat down with his mom. his mom helped him with the pāper. when they were done, his mom said, "this pāper rēads very well. you did a good job."

sam said, "that's good. now let's make a lot of these pāpers so we can give one to everybody who wants one."

the next dāy sam gave ēach boy and girl a pāper. he tōld them to rēad the pāper and do what it said.

now there are many tent kites

flȳing ōver the park. and no one says, "hō, hō." the tent kites flȳ better than any other kite.

the end

82

tim and his hat

tim had a hat. it was red and white. tim said, "I hate this hat." but his mother said, "it is cōld outside. so you must havₑ a hat."

whₑn tim was outside, he said, "I will take this hat and hide it." so he did. he found an ōld trēē with a hole in it. he stuck the hat in the hole. then he said, "whₑn I come back from school, I will get mȳ hat from the trēē."

tim got to school on time. he began rēₐding his book. then he looked out the windōw. what do you think was falling from the skȳ? snōw was falling. whₑn tim saw the snōw, he said, "wow, it is getting cōld out therₑ." and it was. it was getting cōlder and cōlder.

when school was ōver, the snōw was very dēep. tim walked outside. then he said, "mȳ ēars are getting cōld. I had better run home." so tim began to run. he ran as fast as he could go, but the snōw was very dēep and it was hard to run in that snōw. the other boys and girls were plāying in the snōw, but tim did not have time to plāy. he said, "I must get home before mȳ ēars get too cōld."

at last, tim came to the ōld trēe. he grabbed his red and white hat. he slipped the hat ōver his ēars. then he said, "I dōn't hate this hat. I like this hat now."

tim did not hate his hat after

that dāy. and he did not hide his hat
in trēēs. now tim has time to plāy
with the other boys and girls when
the snōw gets dēēp.

this stōry is ōver.

the fox wants a cone

a little girl was sitting in the woods. she had an ice crēam cone. she was sitting on a log, ēating her ice crēam cone.

a slȳ fox was looking at her. that fox was thinking. "I will con that girl. I will con her into giving me her cone."

so the slȳ fox ran up to the girl. then he fell ōver and began to shout, "help me, help me. mȳ mouth is on fire. givе me something cool for mȳ mouth."

"close your eyes and ōpen your mouth," the girl said.

the slȳ fox was thinking, "hō, hō, I connеd that girl out of her cone."

when the fox closed his eyes, he

did not get a cone in his mouth. he
got a drink of cōld water.

"there," the girl said. "that
should make your mouth cool."

"no, no," the fox shouted. "mȳ
mouth nēēds something cōlder than
that water."

the girl said, "close your eyes
and ōpen your mouth."

the fox said to himself, "this
time I will con her out of her
cone."

but he did not con her out of a
cone. he conned her out of a bit of
ice. she dropped the ice into his
mouth. then she said, "now your
mouth must fēēl cool."

"no, no," the fox yelled. "I nēēd
a cone."

the girl said, "you can have the cone, but I ate all the ice crēam."

but the fox did not take the cone. she had made him so mad that he ran back into the woods. he never trĪed to con her again.

more to come

rēad the Ītem

sāy "what" when the tēacher says "that."

the con fox

the slȳ fox wanted an ice crēam cone. he couldn't con the girl out of her cone, but he had a plan. he said, "I will go to the ice crēam stand. when I get there, I will con somebody out of a cone."

so that fox went to town. when he came to the ice crēam stand, he said, "hand me a cone."

the man at the stand made up a big cone. then the man said, "that will be one dime."

the fox said, "but I gave you a dime."

the man said, "no, you did not give me a dime. I think you are trȳing to con me."

"I dōn't con men," the fox said. "I

came here for a cone. and I gave you a
dime for that cone."

the man looked at that slȳ fox. then
the man said, "if this is not a trick, I will
give you the cone."

the fox said, "I am not lȳing. I am
not trȳing to con you."

just then a little girl came up to the
ice crēam stand. it was the girl that the
fox had met in the woods. the girl said to
the fox, "you are the fox that trīed to
con me out of mȳ cone. I am glad to
see that you are buȳing a cone."

the man at the stand said, "so you
are a con fox."

the fox was so mad that he ran back
to the woods. he never trīed to con the
man at the cone stand again.

this is the end.

cones

rēad the Ītem

sāy "spot" if the tēacher says "stop."

don was sad

don had a job that he did not like. he worked in a hat store. he mopped up in that store at the end of ēach dāy. every dāy he mopped and mopped. when he mopped, he talked to himself. he would sāy, "I hate to work in this hat store. I hate to mop."

then he would think of things that he would like to do. he said, "I wish I was big. I wish I could flȳ. I would like to be a super man. but I am just a mopper. I am not big. I cannot flȳ."

when the store was mopped, don would sit and mope. he would think of the things he would do if he was a super man.

"I would fīnd crooks," he said. "they would shoot at me, but I would not fēēl a thing."

every dāy was the same. don would mop and mop. then he would mope and mope. when he mopped, he would think about being a super man. when he would mope, he would think about that too.

then one dāy something happened. don was mopping in the back of the store. all at once, he stopped mopping. "I think I hēar something," he said.

the sound came from the dōōr that led down the stāirs. somebody was sāying, "come down the stāirs." don ōpened the dōōr and went down the stāirs.

to be continued

rēad the Ītem

when the tēacher says "what," sāy "that."

don mēēts a woman

wherₑ did don work?

whȳ did don mope?

somebody tōld don to come down the stāirs. so don droppₑd his mop and went down the stāirs. it was very dim down therₑ. but don could see a woman in the dark. the woman had a cap and a cape. she said, "don, do you want to be a super man?"

"yes, I do," don said.

the woman said, "I will help you be a super man if you tell me that you will do good."

"I will do good," don said.

then the woman handed don a dime. that dime lookₑd dim in the dark.

the woman said, "kēēp that dime. when you want to be a super man, tap the dime thrēē times."

don looked at the dime, but when he looked up, he did not see the woman. "where are you?" don asked.

there was no answer. don called again, but there was no answer. then don took the dime and went up the dim stāirs. he said to himself, "I must be having a drēam." but then he looked at the dime and said, "if I am drēaming, how did I get this dime?"

don picked up his mop and began to mop again. then he said, "I think I will tap that dime thrēē times and see what happens. I hope it works."

so don dropped his mop and tapped his dime one time, two times, thrēē times.

to be continued

read the Item

If the teacher says "for," say "Of."

don Is a Super man

Who gave don a dime?

Where was the woman with the cape
and the cap?

how could don be a super man?

don said, "I hope this works." Then he
tapped the dime one time, two times, three
times. There was the sound of thunder.
"boooooommmmmm."

"What was that?" don asked. he looked
at his hand. The dime was still there. Then
don saw that he had a cape and a cap.
"Wow," don said. "When I tapped that
dime, I became a super man."

don said, "I must keep this dime. I will
tape it to my arm." and he did. Then he

said, "now I will see if I am a super man."

don kicked the wall. "Pow." he made a big hole in the wall. don smiled. "Wow," he said. "I am a super man." he hopped around the store.⑤

he hit the wall again. "Pow." he made another hole in the wall. now there were two holes in the wall.

don hopped around the hat shop hitting things. he said, "I hate hats."

"Pow." he hit a hat box and made a hole in it. Then he said, "I hate mops." So he broke the mop.

"This is fun," he said. by now the store was a mess. There were holes in the wall. The hats had holes in them. The doors had holes in them.

don said, "no one can stop me now. I am a super man."

To be continued

read the Item

When the teacher says "Saw," say "Was."

don has Super fun

Who gave don the dime?

Where did he tape the dime?

Was he doing good things?

did don mope after he became a super man?

don was hopping around the store in his cap and his cape. he was hitting the walls and making holes. he was having a lot of fun.

all at once he stopped. he said, "I will go outside and show what a super man I am."

When don left the store, he didn't open the door. he ran into the door. "Crash."

Some boys were standing outside the store. They said, "look at that funny man in a cap and a cape."

don said, "I am no funny man. I am

★ a super man."

don ran to a car that was parked near the store. he picked the car up and gave it a big heave. The car crashed into another car. ⑤

The boys yelled, "let's get out of here. That man is a nut."

"Come back," don shouted. "let me show you how super I am."

but the boys did not come back. They ran as fast as they could go.

don said, "I think I will fly to the top of this store." So he did. Then he said, "I think I will dive down to the street." So he did. he took a dive. "Crash." he made a big hole in the street.

"This is a lot of fun," don said.

To be continued

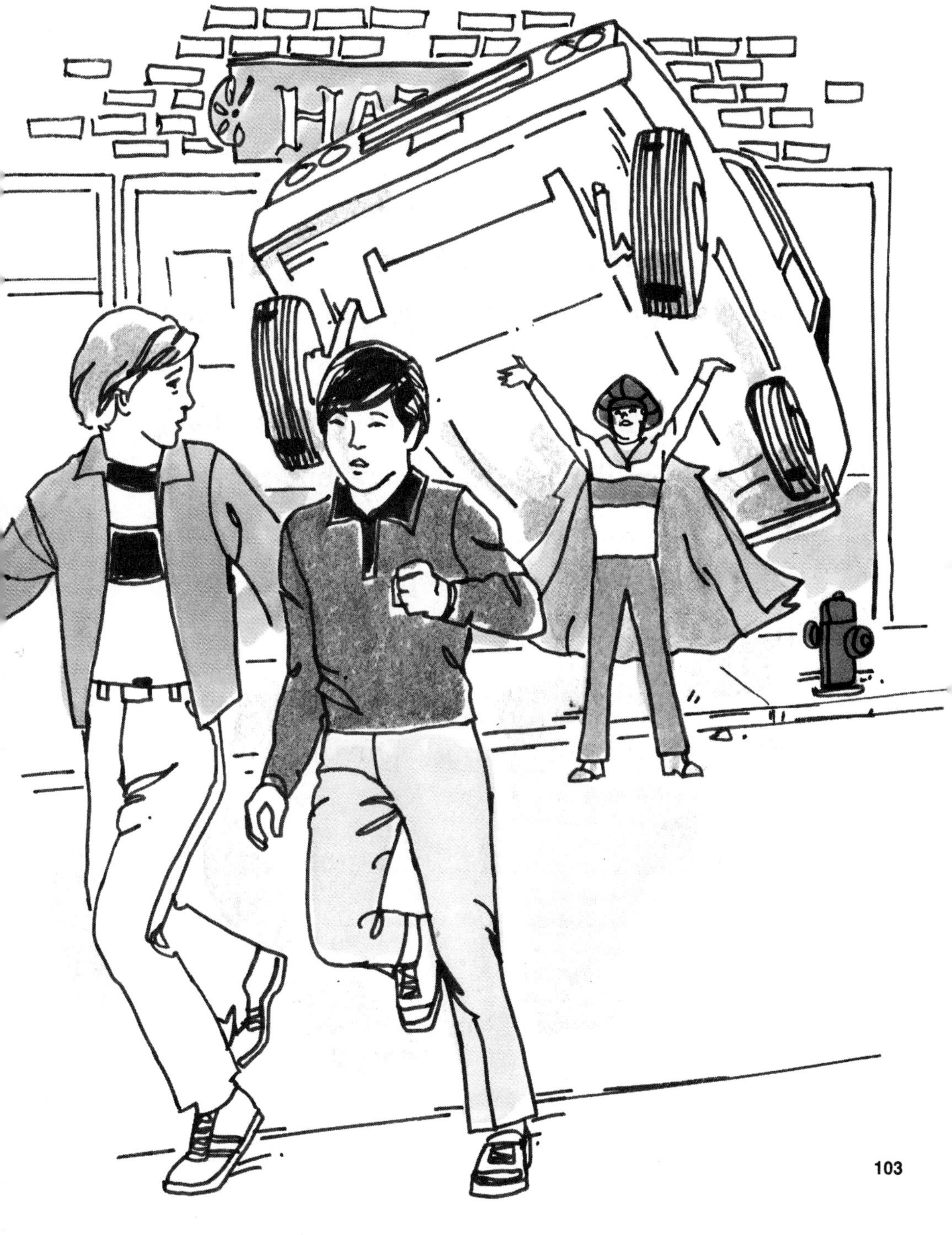

read the Item

If the teacher says "Of," say "for."

don makes a mess

The woman who gave don the dime told him that he was to do good. but was don doing good?

don said, "When I worked in the hat store, I would mope and mop. but now I can have fun. I can fly. I can pick up cars and throw them around. I can do anything I want."

don walked down the street. a man said, "look at that funny man in the cap and cape."

That made don mad. he stopped and said, "I have this cape and this cap because I am a super man."

The man said, "You don't look like a super man to me."

don walked over to a bus. he picked up the bus. Then he gave it a heave. "Crash." The bus was bent.

The man said, "let me out of here." and he ran down the street.⑤

"Come back," don shouted, but the man kept on running.

don walked to a school. boys and girls were coming out of the school. don said, "boys and girls, I am a super man."

One girl said, "You look like a nut in that cap and cape."

a boy said, "let's see how fast you can run."

"I will show you," don said.

he ran so fast that the boys and girls could not see him. "Crash." don ran into the school and made a big hole in the side of the school.

One of the boys said, "Stop that. You

are making a mess out of our school. I
don't like you."

"but you must like me," don said. "I
am a super man, and the boys and girls
love super men."

"We hate you," all the boys and girls
said. Then they ran away. don was sad. he
sat down and began to mope.

To be continued

read the Item

If the teacher says "When," say "Then."

don mopes

The woman in the hat store told don to do good. but did don do what the woman said?

don had made holes in walls. he crashed a car and a bus. he ran into the side of a school. The boys and girls began to shout, "We hate you." Then they ran away.

don began to mope. he said, "I am a super man. but nobody likes me." a tear ran down don's cheek. Then another tear ran down his cheek.

all at once don looked down and saw that he did not have his cape. There was no cap on his head.

don said, "I must see if I am still super."

don ran to the street as fast as he could go. but he did not go very fast. he stopped at a parked car and tried to pick it up. he could not do that.⑤

"I am no longer super," he said. "I will tap the dime again." but the tape and the dime were not on his arm.

Slowly, don walked back to the hat store. he was very sad. he said, "The woman who gave me the dime told me to be a good super man. but I did not do good." It was dark inside the store, but don could see the holes in the walls and the holes in the doors and the holes in the hats.

don sat near the mop and began to mope. "I must fix up this store," he said. he began to clean up the mess when a sound came from the stairs.

"Come down here, don," somebody called.

To be continued

read the Item

When the teacher says "hate," say "hat."

don Works Super hard

Somebody called don from the stairs. don went down the stairs. It was dim down there, but don could see the woman who gave him the dime. The woman had a cap and a cape just like don's.

The woman said, "You did not do good. but I think you are sorry. So I will let you try to be a super man again."

"Oh, thank you," don said. "I will try to be good."

The woman held up the dime. She said, "but before I give you the dime back, you must make up for all the bad things you did."

"I will, I will," don said.

don looked at that dime. When he looked up, the woman was not around. don went up the stairs. he said, "I must clean up the mess I made."

So don began to work super hard.⑤ he fixed walls and doors and hats. Then he mopped up. Then he fixed a car and a bus. Then he went back to the school and began to fix the wall.

When he was done with the wall, a truck stopped in front of the school. a little man began to carry big bags from the truck. The bags were bigger than the man. don jumped up and ran over to the man.

"let me help you," don said. "You are too small for this job."

The man said, "This is the only job I can get. my baby is sick and I must work."

"I will help you," don said.

This is almost the end.

read the Item

When the teacher says "here," say "her."

don does good Things

don helped the little man take big bags from the truck. Then don went back to the store. The woman in the cape and cap was standing inside the store. She handed don the dime and said, "I think you will make a good super man."

don took the dime and said, "Thank you."

Then he taped the dime to his arm. Then he began to tap the dime. When he had tapped the dime three times, "boooooommmmmm" came the sound of thunder. don looked down and saw that he had a cape. and there was a cap on his head. "I am super again," don said.

When he was going out the door, he

stopped and said, "I must do something good." he sat down and began to think. Then he said, "I've got it."

he jumped up and began to fly.⑤ he went this way and that way. he was looking for a truck. When he saw it, he dropped down to the street. he ran up to the truck. The little man was in the truck. don said, "get out of that truck."

The little man got out. "What do you want?" he asked don.

don handed the dime to the little man. "here," don said. "You need this dime more than I do." Then don told the man how the dime works. "Tap the dime three times and you will be a super man. but you must be a good super man."

The man tapped the dime. "boooooommmmmm." he became a super man. and he was the best super man there ever was. he did good things. he fixed things. he worked hard. before long his baby got well, and he was very happy. but he wasn't as happy as don was.

don was no longer a super man. but he did not care. he liked his job. he didn't mope. he was happy because he did the most super thing of all. he helped somebody else.

The end

read the Item

When the teacher says "dime," say "dim."

Sid Worked in a Seed Shop

Sid had a job. he worked in a seed shop. That shop had lots of little plants.

The boss of the shop had a bad leg. So she walked with a cane. When she was not walking with her cane, she left her cane in a big can near the door.

One day the boss said, "I must hop in the truck and go to the other side of town. You stay here and take care of the shop."

So the boss got her cane from the can and went to the truck. When she got in her truck, she said, "There is a pile of notes on the table. Take care of them."★

after the boss left, Sid went to the table and began to read those notes. here is

what one note said. "Send ten pine trees."
but Sid did not read those words. ⑤ here is
what he said, "Send ten pin trees."

Then he looked around the shop for
pins. he stuck the pins in sticks. he made
ten little trees of pins. Then he said, "I
don't know what anybody wants with pin
trees, but I will send them out."

and he did.

Then he picked up the next note. It
said, "fix the window pane." but here is
what Sid said when he looked at the words.
"fix the window pan."

Sid looked around the shop for a
window pan. he said, "I can't see a window
pan, so I will make one." and he did. he
made a big tin pan. he nailed it over the
window. Then he said to himself, "I am
doing a fine job."

more to come

Send ten
pine trees.

read the Item

When the teacher says "her," say "here."

Sid Sends a Con to the farm

Sid did not read well. One note told him to send pine trees. but Sid sent pin trees. another note told him to fix the window pane. but Sid made a window pan.

now Sid went back to the table and picked up another note. The note said, "Tape the oak tree near the door." but Sid did not read the words on the note. here is what Sid said, "Tap the oak tree near the door."

he said, "That seems like a funny thing to do. but I will do it." So Sid went to the oak tree near the door. he tapped it with his hand. Then he went back to the table to read more notes.

here is what the next note said, "Send

a cone to Sam's tree farm."

but here is what Sid said when he looked at the words, "Send a con to Sam's tree farm."⑤

Sid said to himself, "We don't have cons in this shop. Cons are in jail." So Sid called the jail and said to the jailer, "do you have a con that you can send to a tree farm?"

The jailer said, "Yes, we have a fine con. he is getting out of jail today. he needs a job. I will be glad to send him to a tree farm."

"good," Sid said. "Send the con to Sam's tree farm."

after Sid took care of the con, he said to himself, "I am really doing a good job. The boss will be proud of me."

do you think the boss will be proud of the things that Sid has done?

more to come

Tape the oak
tree near
the door.

Read the Item

When the teacher says "Tap," say "Tape."

Sid Plants Seeds in Slop

Sid was reading notes that were on the table. But he was not reading these notes the right way. A note told him to send a cone to a tree farm. But Sid sent a con to the tree farm. Before that he tapped the oak tree near the door. But the note did not tell him to tap the tree. It told him to tape that tree.

Now Sid went back to the pile of notes on the table. He picked up a note that said, "Plant seeds on the slope." There was a slope in back of the shop. That is where the boss planted a lot of little plants. But Sid did not read the note the right way. Here is what Sid said, "Plant seeds in the slop."

Then he said, "These notes are very funny. But I will do what they say."⑤ So Sid grabbed some seeds and went outside. "Where is the slop?" he asked. He looked here and there. Then he saw a big pile of mud near the road. He said, "That must be the slop." So Sid dumped seeds in the mud.

When he was near the side of the shop, a truck stopped in back of the shop. The boss got out of the truck. She was walking with her cane. The boss said, "What are you doing out here?"

Sid said, "I just planted seeds in the slop."

The boss looked at Sid. Then the boss asked, "What did you do?"

Sid told her. The boss got mad. "Not in the slop," the boss yelled. "On the slope. Plant the seeds on the slope."

Sid felt very sad.

More to come

Seeds

Plant seeds
on the slope.

LIN'S
PLANT
SHOP

Read the Item

When the teacher says "Cone," say "Con."

The Boss Gets Mad

Sid was sad and the boss was mad. The boss yelled at Sid for planting seeds in the slop. When the boss was tired of yelling, she said, "Let's go to the shop and see how well you did the other things the notes told you to do."

So Sid and the boss went to the shop. The boss dropped her cane into the can. She went to the table and picked up a note. Then she said, "Did you send out ten pine trees?"

"Pine trees?" Sid asked. "I sent out pin trees."

That made the boss mad. She walked around the room. Then she said, "I hope that you did a better job with the other notes."

She picked up another note. Then she said, "Did you fix the window pane?"

"Window pane?" Sid asked. "I made a window pan."⑤

The boss got her cane from the can. She walked around the room. She yelled and yelled. Then she said, "I hope you sent a cone to Sam's tree farm."

"No," Sid said. "I sent a con from the jail."

The boss sat down on the floor. "This is a fine mess," she said. Then she asked, "Did you tape the oak tree?"

"No," Sid said. "I tapped the oak tree." Sid was very, very sad. He wanted to do a good job, but he didn't read what the notes said.

More to come

Fix the window pane.

Read the Item

If the teacher says "Pin," say "Pine."

The Boss Teaches Sid to Read

Sid felt so sad that a tear ran down his cheek. The boss was so mad that she was sitting on the floor, tapping her cane and looking at Sid. The boss said, "You didn't plant seeds on the slope. You planted seeds in the slop."

"Yes," Sid said. "I didn't mean to do a bad job. But I don't read very well."

The boss said, "Well, I will teach you how to read. If you are going to help me in this shop, you must be good at reading."

So the boss began to teach Sid how to read words like pane and rode and tape and time. Sid sat at the side of the boss and the boss made notes for Sid to read. At first, Sid did not read the words like hope and rob. But every day, Sid would read a little better.⑤ And before a week went by, Sid could read the words very well. The boss made up some hard notes. One note said, "Hide a bit of cheese near the mop." Another note said, "Tape a cap to my cape." But the boss could not fool Sid.

Now, when the boss leaves the shop, she says, "Sid, read the notes on the table and do what the notes tell you to do." That's what Sid does. If a note tells him to fix a window pane, he does it. If a note tells him to send a cone to a tree farm, he sends a cone, not a con. Sid is very happy and so is the boss.

The end

hop hope rob robe

The Tame Tiger Who Liked Ice Cream

There once was a tame tiger. This tiger did not bite children. He didn't eat goats or sheep. He said, "I like ice cream. So I will go to town and get some."

But the tiger didn't have any cash. He said, "I will fill my pouch with round stones. I hope that the man at the ice cream store likes round stones."

So the tiger filled his pouch with round stones. Then he walked to town. He went up to the man at the ice cream stand.

"I don't have any cash," the tiger said. "But I have a pouch filled with pretty round stones."

"Let's see them," the man said.

So the tiger showed the man his stones. The man said, "I like those stones. They are pretty."

The tiger gave the pouch to the man.⑤

Then the tiger said, "I want a big cone, and I want some string."

The man said, "What will you do with a big cone and some string?"

"Wait and see," the tiger said.

What do you think the tiger did? He ate the ice cream from the cone. Then he put the big cone on his head with a string.

The tiger said, "I love ice cream and I love hats. I ate the ice cream and now I have the best hat in town."

The man at the ice cream stand said, "That tiger is very tame. He is also very smart."

The end

Boo the Ghost

There was a big old house near the town. Six ghosts lived in that old house. And five of those ghosts were very mean. They liked to play tricks on boys and girls. They liked to scare people.

Every night after the sun went down, those five ghosts would say, "What can we do that is mean?" The five ghosts would name some mean things.

Then the five ghosts would go out to do mean things. Sometimes they would hide on a dark street. When a child walked by, they would jump out and say, "Oooooow." The child would run and they would say, "Ho, ho."

Sometimes they would go to a farm and make the horses so scared that the horses would run from the barn. The farmer would come out to see what had happened. The ghosts would hide.⑤ When he was near the barn, they would all jump at him and say, "Oooooow." And the farmer would run back into his house.

Five ghosts were mean. But the other ghost who lived in the old house was not mean. His name was Boo. He didn't like to scare horses. Boo liked to ride on horses. He didn't like to scare small boys and girls. He liked to play games with them. He didn't like to do mean things. He liked to do things that made everybody happy.

But the people in town were afraid of him. Farmers were also afraid of him. Boys and girls were also afraid. But the ghosts that he lived with were not afraid of him. They didn't like him. They said, "You are not a good ghost because you are not mean."

More to come

136

Boo Leaves the House

Boo was a ghost, but he was not mean like the other ghosts that lived with him. Those five ghosts were very mean and they liked to do mean things. But Boo was not mean. While the other ghosts went out to do mean things, he would read.

Then one night, the other five ghosts made Boo leave the old house. They came back from playing mean tricks. Boo was sitting in his seat reading a book. The other ghosts said, "You are not a good ghost, so you must leave this house."

"Where will I go?" Boo asked.

"We don't care where you go," the biggest ghost said. "Just get out of this house."

So Boo picked up his heap of books and left the old house. As he walked from the house, he could hear the other ghosts talking and laughing. They were planning to do mean things.⑤

Boo walked down the road. When he was near the town, he stopped. "I hear somebody crying."

Boo looked around in the dark. At last he came to a stream and saw who was crying. It was a big green frog. The frog looked at Boo and stopped crying. The frog said, "Are you really a ghost?"

"Yes," Boo said. "And are you really a talking frog?"

"No," the frog said. "I am a king, but a monster cast a spell over me and turned me into a frog. I am very sad."

"Can I help you?" Boo asked.

"No," the frog said. "Nobody can help me now."

More to come

Boo Goes to the Castle

The five mean ghosts had made Boo leave the old house. When Boo was walking to town, he found a talking frog. The frog was near a stream. But the frog was not really a frog. It was a king. A monster had cast a spell on the king and turned him into a frog.

"I will help you," Boo said. "Just tell me where the monster stays."

The frog said, "The monster is in my castle. That castle is on the other side of town."

"You wait here," Boo said. "I will be back."

Boo floated up into the sky. He floated over the town like a bird. Soon he came to the castle ★ on the other side of town. When he floated near the castle, the hounds began to howl. Boo floated to the top of the wall that went around the castle.⑤ The hounds were howling and howling.

Then the door to the castle opened and out came the meanest-looking monster Boo had ever seen. That monster roared, "Who is out here? Who is making my hounds howl?"

Boo did not say a thing. He just watched the monster.

The monster roared, "If you don't leave, I'll get you. I'll turn you into a frog or a toad."

When the monster went back into the castle, Boo floated from the wall. He found a window and went inside the castle. He could see the monster. Boo said to himself, "That monster is really mean."

The monster was holding a gold rod. She was saying, "As long as I have this magic rod, I can cast a spell over anybody. I can turn anybody into a frog or a toad."

Boo said to himself, "I must get that magic rod from the monster."

Stop

Boo Gets a Fish Tail

Boo was inside the monster's castle. The monster had a magic rod that was made of gold. The monster was saying that she could cast spells on people as long as she had the magic rod.

Boo said to himself, "I must get that rod from the monster."

Boo said, "I will try to scare the monster." So Boo made himself as big and as mean as he could. But he was still pretty small and he didn't really look mean.

He floated down at the monster. "Oooooow," he said.

The monster laughed. "What's this?" she said. "A little ghost thinks he can fill me with fear. I'll show him some fear."

The monster held up the magic rod. "Bod bode, bed bead," she said. All at once, Boo felt funny. He looked down and saw that he had the tail of a fish. ⑤ He had a big fin growing from his back.

"That should hold you for a while," the monster said, and she began to laugh. "Now get out of here before I turn you into a leaf."

Boo really got out of there, because he was really scared. When he was far from the castle, he stopped and looked at himself. He was part fish and part ghost. He wanted to cry. But he didn't cry.

He said to himself, "I must think of some way to get that gold rod from the monster. If I get the rod, I could turn myself back into a real ghost. But that gold rod is my only hope."

Boo sat and began to think. He needed a plan. He sat for a long time. Then all at once, he said, "I have a plan now. And I think it will work."

Stop

Boo's Plan Works

Boo had a plan for getting the gold rod from the monster. Boo floated back to the old house where the other ghosts stayed. He floated inside the house. The other five ghosts were eating their big meal. They always ate a big meal before they went out to do mean things.

When the ghosts saw Boo, they stopped eating and said, "What are you doing here? We made you leave this house. So get out."

Boo said, "I am here because I have found somebody you can't scare."

The five ghosts jumped up from the table. The biggest ghost made himself as big as a horse. Then he made himself look meaner than the monster. "I can scare anybody," he shouted.

The other ghosts made themselves look big and mean, too. "We can scare anybody," they said.

"No, you can't," Boo said.⑤ "There is a monster near here who is so mean that you can't scare her. And she can do magic things. Look at what she did to me."

The five ghosts looked at Boo's fish tail and his fin. They started to laugh.

"That monster can play magic tricks on you," the biggest ghost said. "But you are not much of a ghost. Her magic won't work on us. We are real ghosts."

"No," Boo said. "She will turn you into a log or into a frog.

"Come on," one of the ghosts said. "Let's go get that monster. Let's see her try to play tricks on us."

The other ghosts said, "Yes, let's go. Lead us to her."

Had Boo's plan worked?

Stop

The Ghosts Meet the Monster

Boo was leading the way to the monster's castle. The biggest ghost said, "I'll scare her so much she'll turn into a mouse." Another ghost said, "I'll scare her so much she'll turn into a bug."

Soon, Boo and the other ghosts came to the castle. The hounds began to howl. One of the ghosts floated down near the hounds. He made himself as big as a horse. Then he said, "Eeeeeeeeeee." The hounds ran away like a flash.

Then the ghosts floated into the castle. The monster was sitting at one end of a long table. The gold rod was at the other end. One of the ghosts rammed into the table and broke the table into a thousand bits. Another ghost picked up the monster's plate and heaved it at the monster. "Plop." It hit her in the nose.

Another ghost got behind the monster and made a loud sound.⑤ "Rrrrr." When the monster turned around, the biggest ghost flew at the monster and knocked her down. All of the ghosts were howling and making themselves look as mean as they could.

The monster got up. "What's going on here?" she shouted.

Then all five ghosts flew at her.

"I'm leaving," the monster said. And she ran away from the castle as fast as she could go.

The biggest ghost flew over and grabbed the gold rod.

"This must be a magic rod," he said. "We can have a lot of fun with this rod. We can turn Boo into a leaf."

"That's a fine plan," the other ghosts said.

Stop

The Ghosts Turn on Boo

The biggest ghost had the magic rod. He was going to turn Boo into a leaf. He held the rod and said, "Turn Boo into a leaf." But nothing happened.

"This thing doesn't work," the biggest ghost said.

Another ghost looked at the rod and said, "You're not saying the right words. You have to say funny words if you want to cast a spell. Say something funny."

The biggest ghost said, "Bine bin, fine fin." Nothing happened to Boo. But the biggest ghost turned into a big red flower. The other ghosts laughed. "That was a good trick," they said.

One of the other ghosts grabbed the rod. He said, "I never did like that big ghost anyhow. Now I'm the biggest ghost and I will make this magic rod work for me."

He held the rod and said, "Tim time, cop cope."⑤ Nothing happened to Boo, but the ghost who was holding the rod turned into a leaf.

The other mean ghosts laughed and laughed. Then one of them picked up the rod and said, "Now I am the biggest ghost. And I will find a way to make that rod work."

He held the rod and looked at it for a long time. Then he said, "I see words on the side of this rod. Those words tell how to cast spells."

The other mean ghosts said, "Well, read the words."

The ghost who was holding the rod said, "I can't read."

Stop

Boo Casts Some Spells

The ghosts had found words on the side of the rod. The ghost who was holding the rod said, "I can't read." Then he looked at the other mean ghosts. "Who can read these words?" he asked.

"Not me," they all said. Then the three ghosts looked at Boo.

"You can read," one ghost said. "So read these words and tell us how to turn you into a leaf."

Boo said, "Hand me the rod and I will do the best I can."

So the ghost handed the rod to Boo, and Boo looked at the words on the rod. Then Boo held the rod and said, "Bit bite, ben bean."

Nothing happened to Boo, but the other ghosts began to smile. One ghost said, "I don't feel mean anymore."

Another ghost said, "I feel ★ like
playing games with the boys and girls in
town." ⑤

Another ghost said, "Not me. I feel like
going out and helping a farmer milk cows."

Before they left, they turned to Boo
and said, "Thank you for making us feel so
good."

After they left, Boo held up the rod
and said, "Sip dim, dime dup." The flower
turned back into a smiling ghost. And the
leaf turned back into a smiling ghost. They
both gave Boo a kiss and they left for
school.

"We want to read books," they said.

Boo said some magic words to make his
fins and tail go away. Then he said, "Now
I will go find the frog and turn him back
into a king."

More to come

Everybody Is Happy

Boo had turned the mean ghosts into smiling ghosts. Then Boo had made his tail and fins go away. Now Boo was on his way to turn the frog back into a king.

Boo found the frog on a log in the stream. Boo held up the magic rod. "Come to the shore," Boo said, "and I will turn you into a king."

"Hot dog," the frog said. He jumped from the log and swam to shore in a flash.

Then Boo said, "Hog, sog, bumpy log," and the frog turned into a king. The king said, "Hot dog, I'm a king again. Hot dog."

The king ran around, and yelled, and shouted, and laughed, and rolled around in the sand. When the king was tired out, Boo told him how the ghosts had scared the monster into leaving the castle.⑤

Then the king said, "Boo, you must come and live with me in the castle."

"No, no," Boo said, "I couldn't do that."

"Why not?" the king asked.

Boo said, "I, well . . . I, well . . . ." Boo was shy.

The king said, "You must come and live with me. As king of this land, I'm telling you to come and live with me in my fine castle."

So Boo went to live with the king. And he lived with the king for years and years and years.

Things were very good in the land. The people had a good king. The king had a good friend. And all of the ghosts in the land were very good ghosts. The people didn't say, "Let's not go out at night." They said, "Let's go out at night. Maybe we can find a ghost and play games with him. Ghosts are fun."

The end

Ott Is in Genie School

Ott was going to school. He was trying to be a genie, but he did not know many genie tricks.

Genies live in bottles. When somebody rubs the bottle, the genie comes out in a puff of smoke. Then the genie says, "Yes, master, what can I do for you?"

The master tells what he wants, and the genie gets him what he wants. If the master wishes for an elephant, the genie makes an elephant appear. If the master wishes for a bag of gold, the genie makes a bag of gold appear.

But Ott could not do these tricks. That is why he was still going to school. And he was not the best of those who were in school. When their teacher told the genies to make an apple appear on the table, Ott made an alligator appear on the table.⑤ When the teacher told Ott to make gold appear on the floor, Ott made a pot of beans appear on the floor.

Then one day, something strange happened. Ott and the other genies were working at getting into a little bottle. All at once, an old woman ran into the school and ran up to the teacher. The old woman said, "We need more genies. Somebody has found an old yellow bottle that should have a genie in it. But we have not had a genie in that bottle for years and years."

"What about all of our other genies?" the teacher asked. "Why can't we send one of them to the yellow bottle?"

"They are all working," the old woman said. "This is a big year for genies. People have been finding old genie bottles all year. Every one of our genies is working, so we will have to send one of the children from your school to the yellow bottle."

More to come

Ott Takes a Test

Ott was going to genie school. One day an old woman came in and told Ott's teacher, "We need more genies. We must send one of the children from your school to the yellow bottle."

"No, no," the teacher said. "These children cannot go to work as genies. They are not that smart."

The old woman said, "We cannot wait. The girl who found the yellow bottle may rub it any time, and when she rubs it, a genie must come out of that bottle."

The teacher looked at the children who were working to be genies. The teacher said, "I don't know which of these children to pick. None of them would be a good genie."

The old woman said, "I will give the children a test. The child who does the best on the test will go and work in the yellow bottle."⑤

The old woman walked over to the children. "Here is what I want you to do. Make a peach appear on the floor."

All of the children began to say things to themselves. Then peaches began to appear on the floor—one peach, two peaches, three peaches, and then . . . all of the peaches disappeared under a pile of sand. Ott didn't make a peach appear. He made a beach appear.

"Who did that?" the old woman shouted.

Ott didn't say anything because he didn't know that he had made the beach appear.

The old woman said, "We can't wait anymore. I'll just have to pick one of the children." She looked at each of the children. She stopped in front of Ott.

"You," she said to Ott. "You go to the yellow bottle. Do it now."

Ott smiled and made himself disappear in a puff of smoke. He could not hear his teacher yelling, "No, no, not that one. He never does anything the right way."

More next time

Ott Comes Out of the Bottle

Ott was very happy. He was picked to go into the yellow bottle. It was dark inside that bottle, but Ott didn't care. He was waiting for the girl to rub the bottle. That girl's name was Carla. She had found the bottle in a pile of junk. When she found it, she said, "I like that bottle. I will take it home with me."

So now she was on her way home. She was going down Bide Street. She wasn't thinking about what she was doing.

A bunch of bad boys were always hanging around on Bide Street. Suddenly, Carla saw that three mean boys were following her. One of them said, "What do you have in that bottle?"

"Nothing," Carla said, and she kept on walking.

One of the boys said to the other boys, "Let's take that bottle and bust it."⑤

The boys all went, "Ho, ho, ho."

Carla stopped and looked at the boys. "You better leave me alone," she said. "Or I'll rub this bottle and a genie will come out and beat you up."

"Ho, ho," the boys said. "That girl can really tell lies. Do you think you can fool us with that silly story about the genie?"

Carla didn't know what to do. She didn't really think that there was a genie in the bottle, but she wanted to scare the mean boys. "If you take one more step, I'll rub the bottle."

"I'm going to take that bottle and smash it," one of the boys said. He reached for the bottle. Carla rubbed the bottle. There was a puff of smoke. The boys stopped. They watched as the smoke became a genie.

More to come

Ott Tells Lies

When the mean boys tried to take the bottle from Carla, she rubbed the bottle and Ott appeared.

Ott said, "Oh, master Carla, what can I do for you?"

Carla said, "Give those boys a spanking."

"Yes, master," Ott said. He sounded smart, but he didn't know how to give the boys a spanking. He could only remember the word banking.

"Well," Carla said at last, "are you going to give them a spanking?"

"Yes," Ott said. "A spanking it will be."

Ott waved his hands. Suddenly, Carla, Ott, and the three boys were in a bank. They were banking.

Carla said, "What kind of a genie are you?"

The boys said, "Let's get out of here," and they began to run from the bank as fast as they could go.

Ott was very sad. He said, ★ "Carla, I am a very old genie.⑤ I have been in the bottle for thousands of years. I have not done tricks for thousands of years."

Ott was telling some big lies. He was not a very old genie. He had not lived in the bottle for thousands of years, and he didn't forget how to do genie tricks. He never was able to do them.

Carla said, "Well, can you get us out of this bank and take us home?"

"Yes, master Carla," Ott said. "That should be easy."

Ott folded his arms. He said some words. Boop.

Suddenly, Ott and Carla were standing in the middle of a big city. Carla looked around. Then she said, "This is not home.

This is Rome. Rome is thousands of miles from my home."

More next time

Ott Is a Very Sad Genie

Carla had told Ott to take her home, but Ott didn't take Carla home. He took her to Rome. Carla was getting mad. She was also getting a little scared. She said, "Please get us home this time."

"I will do my best trick," Ott said. He began to spin around. As he was spinning, he said things to himself. Poof. Suddenly, Carla and Ott were standing in the middle of a forest. Carla said, "You must be the poorest genie there is. Where are we now?"

"I don't know," Ott said. "I will have to read my trick book to see what I did to bring us here."

So Ott began to read his trick book and Carla waited and waited. At last, she said, "Could you bring me something to eat while I'm waiting?"

"Yes," Ott said. "What do you want?"⑤

Carla said, "I would like an apple or a peach."

"An apple and a peach you will have," Ott said. He said some words and what do you think appeared for an apple? An alligator. And what do you think appeared for a peach? A beach.

Carla said, "You are a mess of a genie. I asked for an apple or a peach. All I see is an alligator and a pile of sand."

"I will try again," Ott said. "This time, I will try to get you a hot dog."

Ott said some words to himself. Suddenly, a log appeared. The log was on fire. Carla began to laugh.

"That is not a hot dog," she said. "That's a hot log."

Ott was not laughing. He was very sad. He was very poor at being a genie.

More about Ott and Carla next time

Carla and Ott Can't Get Home

Ott and Carla were in a forest. When Ott tried to get a hot dog for Carla, a hot log appeared. Carla laughed, but Ott felt very sad. Carla said, "Can you call for help? If someone hears us, they can tell us which way to go."

"Yes," Ott said. "I will make a sound that is very loud—very loud." Ott said some words to himself. But there was no loud sound. There was a cloud. Again Carla laughed.

She said, "You tried to make something that was loud, but you made a cloud. So why don't you try to make a cloud? Maybe then you'll make a sound that is loud."

"Yes, master," Ott said. He folded his arms and said some words. Suddenly a loud sound filled the air. "Help, help."

Ott said, "It worked. When I tried to

make the cloud, I made a sound that is loud."⑤

Then Ott jumped up and down. He shouted and laughed. Then he said, "I've got it. I've got it. I know how to get us home."

"How?" Carla asked. "How?"

"Well," Ott said, still hopping up and down a bit. "When I wished us to go home, we went to Rome. So if I wish us to go to Rome . . . ."

"We will go home," Carla said. She ran over and gave Ott a kiss.

Ott blushed. Then he folded his arms and said some words. Suddenly, Carla seemed to be flying in the air. And then she stopped and looked around.

"Oh nuts," she said. "We're not at home. We are back in Rome."

Ott said, "I don't know how I do that."

More of this story next time

Ott Disappears

Carla was sad. She felt a tear streaming down her cheek. She said, "You are not a very funny genie. Can't you see that I want to go home? I don't want to stay in forests and get logs that are on fire. I don't want to be standing in the middle of Rome. I just want to go home. Do you hear me?"

Ott said, "I'm really very sorry, master." Now a tear was streaming down Ott's cheek. "I must tell you something," he said. "I told you a lie. I am not a very old genie. I have not been resting in that bottle for thousands of years. I am not old and wise. I am still going to genie school."

Carla said, "Well, isn't there some way to get out of this mess? Can you call for help?"

"Yes," Ott said. "That is one of the things I can do."⑤

Ott folded his arms and said some things to himself. Then Carla could see something flying across the sky. Suddenly it began to dive down to Ott. It came closer and closer. Now Carla could see that it was a big, wet fish. Splat. It hit Ott in the face.

Carla said, "You can't even call for help. You're not much help as a genie at all. In fact, I wish you would get out of here."

"Yes, master," Ott said with a tear running down his cheek. Slowly a puff of smoke formed, and slowly Ott disappeared into the smoke. Then the smoke began to flow into the yellow bottle.

Carla picked up the bottle and tossed it as hard as she could. Crash. It went through the window of a house.

More to come

Ott Helps Carla

Carla picked up the bottle and tossed it through the window of a house. Then a big woman came out, holding the bottle. "Who tossed this bottle through my window?" she screamed.

She ran over and grabbed Carla. "You did it, didn't you? You are the one who tossed that bottle through my window."

"Yes, I did," Carla said. "But I didn't mean to. I didn't . . . ."

"I'll show you," the woman said. She put the bottle down. Then she picked up a broom. She was going to spank Carla with the broom.

Carla bent over and rubbed the bottle. Poof. Ott was back.

He said, "I will try to get you out of this, master." Ott said some words. Suddenly the pane of glass in the window was not broken.

"Stop," Carla said. "Look at your window. It is no longer broken."

The woman looked at her window.⑤ "I don't believe it," she said to herself. "I saw the glass go flying this way and that way. Now the glass is back in the window."

The woman dropped the broom and went back into her house. After she left, Carla gave Ott a big hug. "You did it," she said. "You wanted the window to have a pane of glass and you made it happen."

Ott smiled. "I think I'm getting better at being a genie."

Carla said, "Maybe you can get us out of here now."

"I will try very hard," Ott said. "And please, master, don't hate me if I don't do well."

Carla looked at Ott and smiled. "Okay," she said.

More to come

Carla Reads the Genie Book

Carla and Ott were in Rome. Ott had just made something happen the right way. He had wished for a window pane, and the pane came.

"I think I can get us out of here," Ott said. "But maybe I should call for help. I think I can do that now."

"All right," Carla said. "Call for help." Ott folded his arms and began to say things to himself. Then something began to fly across the sky. It began to dive at Ott. "Splat." It was a big wet, fat fish.

Carla began to laugh. Then she said, "I don't think you're a genie yet."

"You are right," Ott said. Then he held up a big book. "This is my school book," he said. "It tells you how to do things like a genie. Maybe we can read the book and find out how to ★ go home."⑤

"Good plan," Carla said. "Let's go to a

park and sit down in the shade."

So Ott and Carla went to a park. They sat near a little stream.

Carla said, "Let's flip to the back of the book. That part will tell how to do the hard tricks."

So Carla flipped to the back of the book. She stopped at the part that said, "How to Go Home."

"This is what we want," Carla said. She began to read the part out loud.

More next time

Carla Goes Home, Home, Home

Carla was reading from Ott's school book. She was reading a part that told what to do if you wanted to go home. Here is what the book said:

"If you want to go home, fold your arms. Then say the name of your street. Then say the name of your mother. Then say, 'Ib, bub, ib, bub, ib, bub, bibby. Bome, bome, bome. I want to go home, home, home.'"

When Carla was through reading, she said, "Did you hear that, Ott? It told you everything you have to do to get home."

Ott said, "That is too much to remember. I can't remember all of that."

"Oh, it's not so much. Here. I'll read it again, and I'll show you the things you have to do."

Carla began to read to herself. Then she folded her arms and said, "First you say the name of my street and the name of my mother.⑤ Here I go: Oak Street . . . Marta Flores."

Ott stood up and folded his arms. Then he said, "Oak Street . . . Marta Flores."

Carla said, "Here is what you say next: Ib, bub, ib, bub, ib, bub, bibby. Bome, bome, bome. I want to go home, home, home."

Suddenly, Carla was flying through the air. Thud. Now she was sitting on her front steps. She was still holding the genie school book.

"Wow," Carla said, "I did that trick all by myself." She began to think of the wonderful tricks she could play just by reading the genie book.

Suddenly, Carla remembered Ott. "Oh, my," she said. "He is not here. Maybe something bad happened to him. I better call for help."

Carla began flipping through the school book. She stopped at a part that told how to call for help.

More to come

Carla Calls for Help

Carla was reading a genie book. The book told about many tricks. One part told how to call for help. Carla was reading that part now. She wanted to call for another genie who could help her find Ott.

Carla stopped reading the part of the book that told how to call for help. Then she folded her hands and said some words. Suddenly, something appeared in the sky. It began to dive down. It was getting closer and closer. Then it stopped. It was an old genie. She stared at Carla. Then she said, "Don't tell me you called for help?"

"Yes, I did," Carla said. "I need help."

"But that is impossible," the old genie said. "You are a human. Everybody knows that a human is not smart. Everybody knows that it is impossible for a human to do the most simple trick."⑤

"That is not so," Carla said. "I don't

know if I can do every trick in that book.
But I called you, and I did the other trick
I tried."

"That is impossible," the old genie said:

"I'll show you," Carla said.

She opened the book to the part that
told how to make a rock into water. After
she was through reading what the book
said, she found a big rock. She told the old
genie to hold the rock on top of her head.

Suddenly, the rock turned into water.
Splash. It flowed all over the old genie. She
began spitting water. She said, "How dare
you. How dare you do a thing like that to
me."

Carla said, "Don't get mad at me. I
called for help. I didn't call you so that we
could get in a fight. I need your help to
find Ott."

Stop

Carla Goes to Genie School

Carla told the old genie that she didn't want to fight with her. She needed her help.

"I will help," the old genie said.

Then the old genie stood on one foot. She said some words. "Poof." There was Ott standing next to the old genie.

"You're back," Carla said. She ran over and gave Ott a big hug.

"But I'm afraid he'll have to come back to school with me," the old genie said. "He is not doing well as a genie. I will try to send another genie. I will take Ott back to school with me."

"No," Carla said. "I don't want another genie. I want Ott."

"But he is not fit to be a genie," the old genie said. "He can't even find his way home."

"I don't care," Carla said. "I want him for my genie.⑤ He's the one who came out of the bottle when I rubbed it. And he's the genie I want."

"But he must go back to school," the old genie said.

"That's all right," Carla said. "I can go to school with him."

"Oh no," the old genie said. "You can't go to our school."

"Why not?" Carla asked.

"Because you are not a genie," the old genie said. "You are a human. And everybody knows that humans can't do very simple tricks."

"Don't say that," Carla said, "or I will turn a thousand rocks into water and you will have to swim home."

"All right, all right," the old genie said. "You can come to genie school, but I don't think you're going to like it."

"Poof." In an instant, Carla and Ott were standing in front of the other children in the genie school.

Stop

Carla Is the Best in Genie School

Ott and Carla and the old genie were in front of the children in the genie school. The old genie said, "This is Carla. She is going to work in this school just like the rest of you."

One of the boys said, "Not here. She can't stay here. She is only a human, and everybody knows that humans can't do any tricks."

Carla snapped her fingers. A rock appeared. She said to the boy who had just talked, "Sit on that rock."

The boy sat on the rock. Carla folded her arms and said some words to herself.

Splash. The boy was sitting in a pool of water.

"Ho, ho," the other children said. "She can do some good tricks. It will be fun to have her in school with us."

So Carla stayed in school. She worked as hard as any of the genies.⑤ And she was the best in the class. When the teacher told the children and Carla how to do a new trick, Carla was always the best at doing the trick. Then she would help the other girls and boys work on the new trick.

Every day, Carla went to school and worked on new tricks. Every day she became smarter and better at genie tricks. Soon, she was ready to become a genie. She was very proud. She was the only human in the genie school. And she was better than anybody else in school. In fact, her teacher said that she was the smartest one he ever had in school.

Then the big day came. This was the day that everyone in school took a vow to be a genie. After taking this vow, they became real genies and went to stay in a bottle.

This was a very big day for Carla, a very big day.

To be continued

Will Carla Take the Genie Vow?

The day had come for everyone in school to take a vow to be a genie. The old genie came to class that day. She had a ring for every new genie.

Before she gave out the rings, she stood in front of the class and said, "Today is your last day in this school. You have worked hard and now you are ready to leave. You are ready to take your place as a genie. But before you take your vow, remember this. It is not easy to be a genie. You must forget about the things that you want to do. You must think about your master. You must do only what your master wants you to do. Not all of you will have good masters. But once you take the genie vow, you must do what genies have done for ★ thousands and thousands of years.⑤ You must obey your master at all times. You must forget about yourself."

The old genie looked at Carla. Carla
looked down. Then she began to cry. She
felt very bad. She liked the genie school,
but she didn't want to spend the rest of her
life in a bottle. She didn't want to forget
about herself and do what her master
wanted her to do. She said, "I can't do it. I
can't take the vow of a genie."

All of the children looked at her. The
old genie patted her on the back. Then the
old genie said, "We don't want you to take
the vow. You are a human, and you should
spend life as a human spends life. I once
told you that you would not like genie
school."

"But I did like it," Carla said. "I just
can't take that vow."

"Carla," the old genie said, "we are
very glad that you came to our school. You
showed us a lot about humans. We won't
feel bad if you don't take the vows. These

vows are for genies, not for humans."

Carla wiped her eyes. All of the children smiled. Carla could see that they were not mad at her. She felt better now.

Stop

Carla and Ott Are Teachers

Carla had worked hard at the genie school. But she couldn't take the vow that the other genies took. She clapped as each new genie got a ring. And she clapped the hardest for Ott. He was the last genie to get a ring.

Then the old genie said, "Here are your jobs. She handed each genie a folded paper. The paper told where the genie would work as a genie. One genie was sent to Alaska. One genie went to China. One genie went to Japan. And one genie went to stay in a yellow bottle that belonged to a girl named Carla.

The genie who got that job was named Ott. Ott was a genie now. He could do all the genie tricks. He had passed all the tests. And he had taken his vow to do what his master wants him to do.⑤

Just when Ott was reading his note,

the teacher ran into the room. He told the old genie, "Five new bottles have been found. We're going to need more genies, but how are we going to train them? I am the only teacher, and I will have to go to a bottle now."

Carla said, "Wait. Ott and I can train the new genies. The school would have two teachers. That means the school could train more genies than it could with one teacher."

The old genie said, "That is a fine plan."

The teacher said, "Yes, that plan is good."

That's what happened.

Now lots of new genies are being trained. And the boys and girls in genie school have good teachers. Ott is a good teacher, because he remembers how hard it was for him to pick up new tricks. Carla is a good teacher because she is very smart.

And Ott and Carla are very, very happy.

And this is the end of the story.

The Turtle and the Frog

Once there was an egg. This egg was on the shore of a pond. It was in the sand. The sun was shining, and the egg was getting hotter and hotter.

Then one day something came out of the egg. Did a chicken come out of the egg? No. Did a little duckling come out of the egg? No. What came out of the egg? A turtle.

That turtle did not know that he was a turtle. He came out of the egg and looked around. Things looked good to him. The sun felt hot. That felt good. He walked to the pond. The water felt good. He went for a swim. That was fun. Then he sat on a log. He grabbed a fly and ate it. That was good.

Then he saw a frog. The frog got up on the log.⑤ Then the frog said, "You are funny-looking."

The turtle did not know what to say. He had never really looked at himself. He didn't feel funny-looking. Now he felt a little sad. He said to the frog, "You look good."

"Yes," the frog said and smiled. "I am good. Watch this." The frog jumped way up and then—splash. He landed in the water.

"Wow," the turtle said. "I like that. I think I'll jump way up and land in the water."

So the turtle tried to jump way up. But he didn't go way up. He slid off the log and landed in the water. When he came up, the frog said, "Ho, ho. You are funny. You can't even jump. Ho, ho."

The little turtle was not going "ho, ho." He was feeling very, very sad. Before he met that frog, things had seemed good to him. But now the pond did not look pretty,

and the sun did not feel good. Everything
seemed sad.

More to come

Flame the Snake

A little turtle was very sad because he could not do things a frog did. The frog could jump way up. But the turtle could not jump at all. The frog got out of the pond and yelled, "Come up here to the land. I want to take a good look at you."

So the turtle came out of the pond. He was wet all over. So the frog could not see that the turtle had tears on his cheeks.

"Ho, ho," the frog said. "You look like a big toenail. You look like the foot of a horse. You look like a joke." The frog jumped up and down on the turtle's shell. "Come on," the frog said. "Take off this hard coat and let me wear it. Then I will look like a toenail."

"I can't take it off," the turtle said.⑤ "That hard coat is part of me."

The frog started to laugh. He laughed

so hard that tears were running down his cheeks. He laughed until the ground around him was wet. And then he laughed some more.

Suddenly, he stopped laughing. Suddenly, he yelled, "Get out of here. Flame the snake is coming." And then—zip—the frog jumped into the pond.

Before the turtle could get into the pond, a long, fat snake came sliding out of the weeds. The snake slid up to the turtle and smiled.

"Hello," the snake said. "My name is Flame. And I need something to eat. Are you good to eat?"

"I don't think so," the turtle said. "I don't think I'm good at anything."

"That is too bad," the snake said. "But maybe you could help me. Have you seen any frogs around here?"

The turtle looked at the smiling snake. He looked at the snake's big mouth. Then the turtle told a lie.

"No," the turtle said, "I have not seen any frogs around here."

To be continued

Flame the Snake Is a Sneak

Flame the snake was looking for something to eat. The turtle said, "No, I have not seen any frogs around here."

Flame smiled and started to slide back into the weeds. Then that snake stopped and said, "I will be back."

The turtle said to himself, "I don't like that snake. I think she is a sneak. I think I will leave." The turtle walked into the pond and began to swim around. Then the frog came over to him. The frog said, "What did Flame say to you?"

The turtle said, "She said that she wanted something to eat."

The frog asked, "Did she say what she wanted to eat?"

"Yes," the turtle said. "She told me that she wanted to eat a frog."

"That is bad," the frog said. "That is very, very bad." The frog jumped from the

pond and sat ★ on an old log.⑤ He shook
his head. "That is bad," he said again.
"Flame is very strong. Flame is very fast.
And she is a sneak. She gives me a big
scare."

Just then, a big mouth shot up to the
log. Snap. It was Flame's mouth. And it
just missed the frog. The frog jumped from
the log, but he landed in the tall weeds.
Flame smiled and began to slide into the
weeds.

Flame said, "Frogs can't jump very well
when they are in the weeds. I think I will
have my lunch now. I think my lunch is
here in the weeds."

"Save me," the frog yelled. "I can't get
away from that snake. Save me."

The turtle shouted, "I will save you."

The turtle began to walk as fast as
he could go. Flame the snake stopped.

"My, my," Flame said. "I see a walking toadstool." Flame was still smiling. "Get out of my way, you silly-looking thing, or I will eat you, too."

The turtle said, "If you don't stop sliding after that frog, I'll bite you on the nose."

Flame smiled and turned away. She seemed to be going back to the log. But suddenly—snap. Like a shot, her mouth came at the turtle.

This story is not over.

STORY **153**

214

A Snake Must Do What Snakes Do

Flame the snake was after the turtle. Her mouth came at the turtle like a shot. The turtle was not fast like a frog, so he could not jump out of the way. The turtle pulled his head into his shell. And just then —bong—the snake's mouth hit the shell.

"Ow, ow," Flame yelled. "My tooth, my tooth. I think I broke my tooth on that hard shell." Flame was sliding this way and that way. "Ow, ow."

The turtle said, "That would not happen if you were a good snake. But you are a sneak."

The snake said, "You are silly. Everybody knows that snakes are sneaks. I am a snake, so I have to be sneaky."

"No," the turtle said. "You do not have to be sneaky. You could be anything you want."

The snake said, "You're nuts.   You

can't be anything you want. Could you jump like a frog? Could you fly like a bird?"

"No," the turtle said, "I can't do those things."

Flame said, "Then why do you think I can be anything I want to be?"

The turtle said, "Maybe you are right. I can't do things that frogs do. I can only do what turtles do. You are a snake, so you must do what snakes do."

"Thank you," Flame said, and smiled. "If you will get out of my way, I'll do what snakes do. I'll go into the weeds and have a frog for lunch."

"Yes," the turtle said. The turtle stepped to one side and the snake began to slide into the weeds. The turtle was sad, but the turtle felt that Flame must do what snakes do.

This is almost the end.

The Frog and the Turtle
and the Snake Get Along

Flame the snake was sliding into the weeds. She was going after the frog.

"Save me, save me," the frog yelled. "Please save me from this snake."

Suddenly, the turtle took a big bite out of the snake's tail. "Ow, ow," the snake yelled. "Why did you do that?" Flame asked. "I must do what snakes do."

The turtle said, "I have to do what turtles do."

Then Flame called, "Frog, oh frog. Come out here." The frog hopped out of the weeds. He looked scared. Flame looked at him and began to slide after him.

"Stop," the turtle called. "Stop, or I will bite your tail again."

So Flame stopped. Then the turtle said, "You can be a sneak when you are not around me or this frog. But you cannot be a sneak around us."⑤

Flame said, "Can I be a sneak when I go to hunt rats near the farm?"

"Yes," the turtle said.

Flame asked, "Can I be a sneak and eat a frog?"

"No," the turtle said. "You must be good to that frog."

Flame looked sad. "I will be good," she said.

So from that day on, the frog and the turtle and the snake got along very well. The frog did what frogs do. He jumped and swam and went "Croak, croak" at night. But that frog did not make fun of turtles any more.

When Flame was not near the pond, she did what snakes do. She would sneak and she would eat many things. But when she was around the frog and the turtle, she was a good snake.

Now the turtle felt good again. He liked to watch the frog jump and watch the snake slide along the ground. He liked the hot sun and the cool water. He liked to be alive.

This is the end.

In the Land of Peevish Pets

Jean was very sad. Her dad would not let her have a pet dog. She said to herself, "I will go to sleep tonight. And I will sleep so hard that maybe I will go to a land that is far away. Maybe I will go to a land where I can have all the pets I want."

So Jean went to bed. She kept telling herself to sleep very hard. "Sleep hard," she said to herself.

And what do you think happened? She went to sleep and began to sleep very hard. She went into the deepest sleep there ever was. She slept and slept. And in her sleep she began to have a dream. There were lots of pets in her dream, but they were not like any pets that Jean had ever seen before. There were funny green animals with big hands and red feet.⑤ There were little bugs that talked. There were strange trees that seemed to be singing. And right in the middle of her dream was an old wizard.

"Ho, ho," the wizard said to her. "What is your name?"

"Jean," she answered.

"Well, Jean," he said, "I hope you have a fine time here in the land of peevish pets. But you must remember this rule: All little crumps are mean."

"What are little crumps?" Jean asked.

"That doesn't matter," the wizard answered. "Just remember the rule: All little crumps are mean."

Jean said, "I'll remember that rule: All crumps are mean."

"No, no," the wizard said. "All <u>little</u> crumps are mean."

"I've got it," Jean said. "But what and when . . . ."

The wizard was gone, and Jean was all alone in the land of peevish pets.

More to come

Jean Meets a Mean Crump

Jean was in the land of peevish pets. She was trying to remember the rule the wizard had told her about crumps. What was that rule?

Jean saw an animal that looked like a frog. She said, "Are you a little crump?"

The animal said, "Gump, gump."

She spotted another animal. It looked like a ball of pink hair. She said, "Are you a little crump?"

The animal answered, "Wup, wup."

Jean asked other animals if they were crumps. But she did not find one crump. Then she said, "I think I will sit down and rest."

Just then, she saw two chairs. One chair was big and the other was little. She said, "I will sit in the little chair."

Just as she was getting ready to sit down, the chair said, "Crump, crump." When it said "Crump," she jumped. And she jumped just in time.⑤ The chair began to run after her.

"That little chair is a little crump," she said. The crump was swinging its arms. It was trying to bite her. She ran as fast as she could go. Suddenly she stopped. The wizard was standing in front of her. She said, "I don't like this place. Get me out of here."

The wizard laughed. He said, "You can't leave this place until you know sixteen rules. You already know one rule. Here is the next rule: If you say, 'Away, away,' a mean crump will go away."

Jean said, "I think I have that rule. If you say, 'Away, away,' a crump will go away."

"No," the wizard yelled. "A <u>mean</u> crump will go away."

Jean said, "But what and when . . . ."

The wizard was gone again. The little crump was sneaking up behind Jean. She turned around and tried to remember what to do, but she couldn't remember the rule.

Tell Jean how to make the mean crump go away.

Jean yelled, "Away, away." What do you think happened? That's right. The little mean crump went away.

More next time

Jean Follows a Dusty Path

Jean was having a strange dream. In her dream, a wizard told her that she must know sixteen rules before she could leave the place in her dream. She already knew a rule about little crumps: All little crumps are mean. She also knew a rule about getting rid of mean crumps. After you say that rule, you can turn this page around and read it.

If you say, "Away, away," a mean crump will go away.

Jean said to herself, "I will walk and walk until I find a way out of this silly place. I wish that wizard was here."

Just then, the wizard popped out from behind a tree. He said, "If you are going to walk around, remember this rule: Every dusty path leads to the lake."

Jean said, "Thank you. I can remember that rule. Every path leads to the lake." ⑤

"No," the wizard said. "Every <u>dusty</u> path leads to the lake."

Jean said the rule to herself. Then she turned to the wizard and said, "But what and when . . . ."

The wizard was gone.

Jean said, "I think I will go to the lake. What was the rule about going to the lake?"

Tell Jean the rule. Say it loud so that she can hear it.

"Thank you," Jean said. "Every dusty path leads to the lake."

So Jean went down a dusty path. Soon she came to the lake. But she didn't like the lake. The water was pink and there were funny animals all around the lake. She said, "I will leave this lake." So she started to walk back down a dusty path.

Do you think that dusty path led away from the lake?

What's the rule?

The path led right back to the lake.
Why?

Yes, the rule says that every dusty path
leads to the lake.

Jean tried to leave the lake by taking
another dusty path. Where do you think
that path led? Why?

Yes, the rule says that every dusty
path leads to the lake. That path was dusty,
so it led right back to the lake.

To be continued

230

Jean Follows a Rocky Path

Jean was mad. And she was tired. She was trying to leave the lake. She walked down dusty paths, but they led right back to the lake.

Tell Jean the rule about dusty paths. After you say the rule, turn this page around and read it.

Every dusty path leads to the lake.

Jean said, "I wish that wizard was around here."

Just then the wizard appeared. He said, "I see that you know the rule about the dusty paths. Now I will tell you the rule about the rocky paths. Every rocky path leads to the mountain."

"I can remember that rule," Jean said. "Every rocky path leads to the mountain."

"Very good remembering," the wizard said. "Soon you will know all sixteen rules."

Jean said, "But what and when . . . ."

Again the wizard was gone. Jean said,
"I want to go to the mountain.⑤ But I can't
remember which path to take."

Tell Jean the rule about the paths that
go to the mountain.

"Oh, thank you," Jean said. She took a
rocky path and soon she came to a big
mountain. But there were crumps all around
the mountain. And some of them were little.
What do you know about little crumps?

Jean said, "Oh, dear. There's a rule
about how to get rid of mean crumps, but
I can't remember that rule."

The mean crumps were starting to run
after Jean. Help Jean out. Tell her what to
do to make the mean crumps go away.

Jean said, "Away." Did the crumps go
away? Why not?

Jean said, "Go away." Did the crumps
go away? Why not?

Jean said, "Away, away." Did the

crumps go away. Why? What's the rule?
After you say the rule, turn this page
around and read the rule.

If you say, "Away, away," a mean crump
will go away.

More in the next story

233

Jean Looks for Food

Jean was dreaming about a strange place. She was at the mountain in the land of peevish pets. And she was very hungry. She said, "I wish I had something to eat, and I wish the wizard was here."

Just then the wizard appeared. He said, "You may eat all you want, but remember this rule: Red food is good to eat. See if you can say that rule."

Jean said, "Red food is good to eat."

The wizard said, "Good remembering."

Jean said, "I will remember that rule. But what and when . . . ."

The wizard was gone again. Jean said to herself, "That is strange. Every time I say 'But what and when,' the wizard goes away."

Jean looked around and found lots of food. There was food on the ground. There was food on the side of the mountain. There

was a bowl of yellow ice cream right in
front of her.⑤ Should she eat that yellow ice
cream?

How do you know?

Tell Jean the rule before she tries to
eat that ice cream. ★

Jean saw big white grapes on a vine.
Should she eat those white grapes?

How do you know?

Tell Jean the rule before she tries to
eat them.

Jean saw a red banana. Should she eat
that red banana?

How do you know?

Tell Jean the rule.

Jean did not think that the banana
looked very good, but she took a bite out
of it.

"Wow," she said. "This is the best
banana I have ever had." She ate that
banana.

Then she found another banana. That banana was yellow. Should she eat that banana?

How do you know?

Tell Jean the rule.

Jean dropped the yellow banana and picked up a red banana. She began eating it.

This is not the end.

Jean Eats Red Bananas

Let's see how much you remember.
What is the name of the land that Jean was
dreaming about?

How many rules did she have to know
before she could leave this land?

She knew a rule about little crumps.
What did she know about all little crumps?

What do you do to make a mean crump
go away?

What kind of path would you take if
you wanted to go to the lake?

What kind of path would you take if
you wanted to go to the mountain?

What kind of food is good to eat?

Jean had eaten a red banana, and it was
very good. She picked up another red banana
and ate it. Then she ate another red banana.
When she had eaten the third red banana,
she looked at her hand. It had red stripes
on it. Her other hand had red stripes, too. ⑤

She said, "What is happening to me?" She looked at her legs. They had red stripes. Her feet had red stripes. She had red stripes all over herself.

She shouted, "Where is that wizard?"

"Here I am," the wizard said, and stepped out from behind a tree.

Jean asked, "Why do I have red stripes all over myself?"

The wizard answered, "There is a rule about red bananas. If you eat three red bananas, you get red stripes."

Jean said, "Why didn't you tell me that rule before? Look at me. I have red stripes all over. I don't want to have red stripes."

"But now you know another rule," the wizard said. "That is good."

Jean said, "But what and when . . . ." Suddenly, the wizard disappeared. Jean was all alone again. She began to rub her arm to get rid of the red stripes. But they wouldn't rub off.

She was very sad. Suddenly something said, "Crump, crump." She turned around and saw a little crump coming after her. Tell Jean how to make that crump go away.

Jean said, "Away, away." And the crump went away. But Jean still had red stripes.

She said, "I hope I remember that rule about eating three red bananas." Help Jean say the rule.

More about Jean's stripes next time

Jean Wants to Get Rid of the Red Stripes

Jean was having a dream. What was the name of the land in her dream?

Was Jean having a good time?

Why did Jean have red stripes all over herself?

What's the rule about three red bananas?

She said, "Oh, I wish the wizard was here." Just as she said the words, the wizard appeared. Then Jean said, "What's the rule about getting rid of all these red stripes?"

The wizard said, "Here's the rule: If you jump in the lake, the stripes will disappear. Can you say that rule?"

Jean tried to say the rule, but she got mixed up. Help her say the rule.

After Jean said the rule, she said, "But what and when . . . ."

The wizard disappeared.

Jean said, "Well, I had better go to the lake."

Jean saw a rocky path. She ran down it as fast as she could go.⑤ Where did the rocky path lead?

Tell Jean the rule about every rocky path.

When Jean came back to the mountain, she remembered the rule about rocky paths. She saw two more paths. One path was muddy. One path was dusty. Tell Jean which path leads to the lake.

"Thank you," Jean said, and ran down the dusty path. Her striped legs were going very fast, and her striped hair was flying in the wind.

To be continued

Jean Makes the Red Stripes Disappear

Why did Jean have red stripes all over?

What could she do to make the red stripes disappear?

So which path was she taking?

Jean ran down the dusty path. Did the path lead to the mountain?

What's the rule about every dusty path?

Soon Jean came to the lake. But there were five little crumps on the path in front of her. Jean said, "I wonder if those little crumps are mean."

Tell Jean the rule about all little crumps.

The crumps began to run after Jean. Jean said, "Oh, my. Oh, dear. Oh, oh. I forgot what to say to make these mean crumps go away."

Tell Jean what to say.

Jean said, "Away, away." And what did the mean crumps do?

What's the rule about making mean

crumps go away?

After the mean crumps went away, Jean jumped into the lake.⑤

Did the red stripes disappear?

What's the rule?

The red stripes disappeared, but now her hair had turned white.

She said, "Oh, my. Oh, dear. I wish the old wizard was here."

Suddenly, the wizard appeared. He said, "Listen, my dear, and I will tell you the rule for getting rid of your white hair. If you stand on one foot, the white hair will disappear."

Jean tried to say the rule five times. But she couldn't do it. Help her out. Say that rule for her.

At last, Jean said the rule. Then she said, "But what and when . . . ."

The wizard disappeared.

To be continued

Jean Makes Her White Hair Go Away

Jean's hair had turned white. The wizard had told her what she had to do to make the white hair go away. What did she have to do?

Tell Jean the rule. See if you were right. Turn the page around and read the rule.

If you stand on one foot, the white hair will disappear.

Jean stood on one foot. Did her white hair go away?

Tell Jean the rule again.

Jean ran over to the lake. She bent down and looked at herself in the water. Then she said, "Oh, no." The white hair had gone away. But now Jean did not have any hair at all. She was bald. She felt the top of her head.

"Oh, no," she said. "I hate this place. I wish the wizard was here so that he could tell me what to do."⑤

Just then the wizard appeared. The wizard laughed when he looked at Jean. She said, "Don't laugh at me. I'm just trying to get out of this place."

The wizard said, "And you are doing a good job, my dear. You must know sixteen rules before you can leave the land of peevish pets. And look at all the rules you know. See if you can answer all of these questions."

Here are the questions the wizard asked:

1. What do you know about all little crumps?
2. How do you make mean crumps go away?
3. What do you know about every dusty path?
4. What do you know about every rocky path?
5. What do you know about red food?

6. What happens if you eat three red bananas?

7. How do you get rid of the red stripes?

8. How do you make white hair disappear?

The wizard said, "You already know eight rules."

Jean said, "I don't care. I want to know how to make my hair come back. I don't like to be bald."

The wizard said, "Here's the rule: If you want your hair back, clap your hands."

Help Jean say that rule.

More of this story next time

A Funny Animal Appears

The wizard told Jean a rule for getting her hair back. Tell Jean that rule.

Jean started to ask the wizard, "But what and when . . . ."

But the wizard disappeared before she could ask the question. Jean said, "I think I'll get my hair back." Jean clapped her hands. So did she get her hair back?

Jean felt her head. Her hair was back. She ran to the lake and looked at herself in the water. Her hair was back, but it was striped again.

She said, "Oh, well. I would rather have striped hair than be bald."

Just then a big, funny-looking animal came out of the lake. Part of that animal looked like a horse, and part of that animal looked like a monkey. The animal walked up to Jean and said, "I can help you get out of this place. I know all sixteen rules."⑤

"Good," Jean said, "Teach me the rules I don't know."

The funny animal said, "Here's a good rule: All dusty paths lead to the mountain."

"No," Jean said. ★ "That's not right. Dusty paths do not lead to the mountain."

The animal looked very angry. He said, "Are you saying that I would tell a lie?"

"No," Jean said.

The talking animal said, "Here is another good rule: If you jump in the lake, you will get red stripes."

"No," Jean said. "If you jump in the lake, the stripes will disappear."

The talking animal looked very angry. "Do not say that I lie. Talking animals never lie. If you don't want to know the rules, I will not tell you any new rules."

Jean said, "Please tell me a new rule. I must know the rules so that I can leave this strange place."

"All right," the talking animal said.
"Here is a good rule: If you want to have
fun, say, 'Side, slide.'"

Help Jean say that rule.

"Thank you," Jean said. "I think I will
have some fun right now."

What can Jean say to have fun?

More next time

Jean Says, "Side, Slide."

What rule did the talking animal tell Jean?

Jean wanted to have some fun, so she said, "Side, slide." But she didn't have fun. All at once, she found herself up to her nose in snow. She was very cold. Snow was falling. The wind was howling. She shouted, "This is no fun. Wizard, where are you?"

The wizard popped out of a pile of snow. "Here I am," he said.

"Get me out of here," she shouted. "I'm cold. I want to be warm again."

Suddenly, the snow disappeared and Jean was warm again. She said, "What happened? I said, 'I want to be warm again,' and I was warm again."

The wizard smiled. He said, "That is the easiest rule in the land of peevish pets. If you want to be warm again, you say, 'I want to be warm again.'" ⑤

Jean said the rule to herself five times. Say it with her.

Then Jean sat down and said to the wizard, "I don't understand something. That talking animal told me a rule about having fun. But the rule didn't work. He said, 'If you want to have fun, say, "Side, slide."' But I said those words, and I didn't have fun."

The old wizard laughed. Then he said, "That talking animal told you the rule for cold. Here's the rule: If you want to be cold, say, 'Side, slide.'"

Jean said, "There are so many new rules that I mix them up. Let's see if I know the right rule. If you want to be cold, say, 'Side, slide.'"

"That is right," the wizard said.

Jean said, "And if you want to be warm again, you say, 'I want to be warm again.'"

"That is right," the wizard said.

Jean said both of those rules to herself

a few times. Then she said, "But why did that talking animal tell me a rule that didn't work? Doesn't he know the rules?"

"He knows them," the wizard said. "But there is a rule about talking animals. I'll ask you some questions. See if you can find out the rule."

The wizard asked, "Did that talking animal tell you the right rule about dusty paths?"

Then he asked, "Did he tell you the right rule about what would happen if you jumped in the lake?"

Then he asked, "Did he tell you the right rule about what would happen if you said, 'Side, slide'?"

Jean said, "I think I know the rule about talking animals."

More to come

Jean Figures Out a Rule

The talking animal had told Jean a rule about how to be cold. But he had told her that it was a rule for how to have fun.

What is the rule about how to be cold?

Then Jean had found out a rule for how to be warm again. Tell Jean that rule. If you don't remember it, turn the page around and read the rule.

If you want to be warm again, say, "I want to be warm again."

Now Jean was trying to figure out a rule about talking animals. She said to herself, "That talking animal lied to me when he told me the rule about the dusty path. He lied when he told me the rule about jumping in the lake. And he lied about what would happen if I said, 'Side, slide.' I think I know the rule about talking animals."⑤

She turned to the wizard. "Here's the rule," she said. "Talking animals lie."

"That's right," the wizard said. "Never believe what a talking animal tells you. If he tells you that pink ice cream is good to eat, you know that pink ice cream is not good to eat. If he tells you that big crumps are very mean, you know that big crumps are not mean."

Jean said, "And if he tells you to eat three green apples, you know you shouldn't eat three green apples."

"That's right," the wizard said. "Now you know a rule about talking animals. Talking animals lie. Don't do what they tell you to do, or you will get in a mess."

"I will remember that," Jean said. "If a talking animal tells me to do something, I will not do it."

Jean ran her hand across her striped

hair. Then she began to ask the wizard a question. "But what and when . . . ." she said.

But the wizard had disappeared. Jean said to herself, "That's strange. Every time I say, 'But what and when . . . .' the wizard disappears."

Just then somebody said, "Hello." Jean looked around, but she did not see anybody.

"I am down here. I am a little bug." Jean bent down and looked at the bug. She said, "Are you a talking animal?"

"No," the bug said. "I never talk."

More next time

She Tricks a Talking Animal

Jean had met a talking bug. She said to herself, "This is a talking animal. There is a rule about talking animals, but I can't remember it." Tell Jean the rule about talking animals.

The bug said, "I will help you get out of here. I know all the rules, and I will tell you the best rules."

Jean had an idea about how to trick the talking animal. She said to herself, "If this animal says that something is fun, it won't be fun. If he tells me that something is good, it won't be good. If he tells me that something is bad, it won't be bad."

Jean smiled to herself. "I will ask him to tell me a rule about something that is really bad. But he won't tell me a rule about something that is bad. He will lie.⑤ He will tell me a rule about something that is good. I will trick him."

Jean said, "I have to find out more about the bad things in this place. Tell me a rule about something that is very, very bad."

The bug smiled and said, "Here's a rule about something that is really bad. If you tap your foot three times, you will turn into a snake."

"Thank you," Jean said. "You are a talking animal and I tricked you. I will tap my foot three times and see what happens."

"Don't do that," the bug cried. "You will be sad. You will be a snake. Don't do it."

Jean tapped her foot three times. Suddenly, she was flying like a bird. The wind was blowing her striped hair. She went down. Then she went up. "Wow," she said. Then she did a loop. "Wow," she said again. "This is more fun than anything."

She began to fly faster. Then she said, "I hope I remember the rule about flying."

What do you do if you want to fly? Tell Jean the rule.

Jean was flying over a town now. She looked down and saw a man that looked like the wizard. So she dropped down to the ground. But the man was not the wizard. He was very strange-looking. He stared at Jean and she stared at him. Then she said, "Hello, my name is Jean."

He said, "Bark, bark."

More to come

The Strange-Looking Man

What did Jean do so that she could fly?

What's the rule?

Who did she see when she was flying?

What did the strange-looking man say to her?

Jean said, "Can't you say anything but 'bark, bark'?"

The man said, "Squeak, squeak."

"I hate this place," Jean said. "I'm sorry that I ever wanted to dream about pets. I haven't seen a good pet in this place. I want to go home."

The man handed Jean a note. The note said, "This man is a pet. He is any kind of pet you want. He can be a cat, or a dog, or a horse, or a pig. Just tell him what kind of pet you want."

Jean looked at the man and said, "Let's see you be a dog." And the man became the word dog. The man became three letters, d-o-g.⑤

"This is too much," Jean said. She began to walk away. The letters d-o-g said, "Bark, bark."

"Oh, be quiet," Jean said. "Dogs don't say, 'Bark, bark.' They say, 'Woof, woof.'"

"Bark, bark," the letters said.

"I wish that old wizard was here," Jean said. "I want to find out more rules so I can get out of here."

Just then the wizard appeared. He said, "You have found out a rule about the man who can become letters."

"Yes," Jean said. "If you tell him to become a dog, he becomes the letters d-o-g."

"Very good," the wizard said. "Remember that rule, because I cannot tell you any more rules. You have to find out the last two rules by yourself."

Jean said, "But what and when . . . ."

The wizard disappeared.

She said, "Darn that wizard. Every time I say 'But what and when,' he disappears."

Suddenly, Jean jumped up. She said, "That's the rule for making the wizard disappear. If you want the wizard to disappear, you say, 'But what and when.'" Say that rule with Jean.

Jean needed only one more rule to leave the land of peevish pets.

This is almost the end.

bark bark

dog

Leaving the Land of Peevish Pets

Jean had found out fifteen rules. The last rule she found out told about making the wizard disappear. She needed only one more rule. So she sat down and began to think. Suddenly, she jumped up. She said, "I've got it. Every time I needed help, the wizard appeared. I think that's the rule. I'll find out." She stood up and yelled, "I need help."

Suddenly, the wizard appeared. Jean said, "I think I know all of the rules. I know how to make you appear. Here's the rule: If you want the wizard to appear, call for help."

"Good," the wizard said.

Then Jean said, "So now I can leave this land of peevish pets."

"That is right," the wizard said. "You have found out all the rules. So you may leave. Just close your eyes."

Jean closed her eyes. Suddenly, she felt something licking her face.⑤

She opened her eyes. She was in bed. Her mom and dad were standing near the bed, and there was a puppy on the bed. He ★ was licking Jean's face. He was black and brown and white. And he had a long tail. He was very pretty. Jean hugged him.

"Can I keep him?" she asked. "Can I, please?"

"He's your puppy," her mom said. Jean hugged the puppy harder. The puppy licked her face again.

Jean's mom said, "Somebody left this puppy for you. There was a note with him."

Jean's dad handed the note to Jean. The note said: "This dog is for Jean. His name is Wizard. And here is the rule about Wizard: If you love him and play with him, he will grow up to be the best dog in the land."

Jean was so happy that tears were running down her cheeks. She said, "Thank you, Wizard. Thank you very much."

She followed the rule, and her dog Wizard did become the very best dog in the land.

This is the end.